small things
SWEET

photography by Battman

Distributed in the United States by Battman Studios
New York, New York

Published by Alan "Battman" Batt, Battman Studios
Text and Photographs © 2009 by Battman
All rights reserved. Printed in China.

ISBN 0-933477-31-7

www.battmanstudios.com

Editor: A J Schaller
Book Design: Lisa Sragg, enmoda design, New York

Camera equipment by Canon / Lighting by Lowel Lighting

Front Cover: Sandro Micheli, Adour Alain Ducasse
Back Cover: Jennifer Giblin, Blue Smoke
Cover Photography: Battman

Restaurants and Chefs

Introduction

Most pastry chefs are very different than savory chefs. They work more meticulously than their savory counterparts. Because of the nature of the food they can be more creative with the presentation. They can make amazing fun shapes. Swirls and curls, molding the food any way they want to. All the garnishes can look like whatever they dream up. They can incorporate many different textures by cooking the same ingredients in different ways. Ingredients like sugar can be liquid or solid, crunchy or smooth. They can make the dessert an infinite number of colors. Although it is very complicated it doesn't appear to be as serious as savory. I had thought about shooting this book on black Plexiglas, like I did with "small things, Savory," to bring out the colors, but it didn't feel right. Dessert is fun, black is serious.

As always, the pastry chefs continue to amaze me with the visuals. Of the 300 or so desserts I've photographed for the last three books, I can not remember one that looked the least bit similar to any other. So enjoy this book. I hope it inspires you to be creative. It certainly has done that for me. It is a great pleasure for me to work with all these wonderful chefs.

Battman

Foreword

Every so often I'll be meticulously scrambling about the kitchen, quenelling chocolate stout ice cream to finish a chocolate peanut dessert, or injecting a fresh rhubarb soda with co2 for a ginger ice cream soda. And in the background I will hear the kitchen phone ringing, practically off the hook, because no one is capable of answering. And when I do get over to answer, "kitchen, can I help you?" I hear, "hey Johnny it's Battman, you wanna do another book?' And I say, "sure, what do you got in mind?" The response is always something that gets the juices flowing, so to speak. In this case creating "small things."

Whether it be a white peach soup with frozen sheep's milk yogurt, or a rich salted caramel ganache truffle, coated in ground sourdough pretzel, the smallest of things can still be big enough to hit all the key aspects of your taste buds. Small things can refer to the small dishes that many pastry chefs come up with as a "palate cleanser" or pre-dessert as we like to call them. Or the last bites, or mignardises, served at the end of the meal with coffee or tea. In either case, the pastry chef usually has one of his or her top team members assembling these dishes, as they may be the very last impression that the guest receives before leaving the restaurant. So we want to make sure that these "small things" get just as much attention as the "big" things do.

I think in this book, you will see all the different renditions of each pastry chef's idea of small things. From the simplicity of a well-made macaron, to the childhood favorite ice cream cone that has been shrunken down to a bite size treat. You'll have every sweet small thing portrayed as only Battman could display.

I've known Battman for about six or seven years now, and I have never met a photographer who is as low maintenance as he. He walks into the restaurant, usually carrying one or two bags, and asks, "where you wanna shoot?" And within what seems to be five minutes, says, "all set". Meanwhile I haven't even figured out which plate I want to use.

In the end, the dishes always end up looking better in his camera than they do in person. And with so little effort, it seems, Battman has not only become a great person to do work with, but also a great friend. I am sure you will love the creative array of colors, shapes and textures that we have all put together and that Battman has translated into a gallery of small things sweet.

Johnny Miele
Pastry Chef, Eighty One

elderflower tempura

7 ounces water

3 ½ ounces elderflower syrup,
if not available use powdered sugar

4 ounces rice flour

12 large fresh picked elderflower blossoms,
two per serving

Olive oil (or preferred oil) for frying

Fresh ground course pepper

Powdered sugar (optional)

cinnamon sugar

1 ounce granulated sugar

1 ounce ground cinnamon

Whisk the water, elderflower syrup, and rice flour until batter is smooth and no lumps remain. Transfer to a large ISI siphon bottle, for whipped cream. Charge with 5 soda chargers (for seltzer water). You also can use 7 ounces of seltzer water for the batter if you don't have soda chargers. Shake well, spray some batter into a bowl, and coat the fresh picked elderflower blossoms into batter.

In a small bowl, mix the sugar and cinnamon together to make the cinnamon sugar. Hold in a dry airtight container until ready to use.

Heat the oil to 350° - 375°F. While holding the end of the blossom, immerse into the hot oil. Shake while frying to help re-open the flower. Remove with a slotted spoon or a fork and drain on paper towels. Sprinkle with cinnamon sugar and fresh ground course pepper. For additional sweetness, sprinkle with powdered sugar.

4

small things SWEET

pastry chef
Alex Grunert

www.bluehillfarm.com

roasted rhubarb

2 long, wide stems of red spring rhubarb

2 tablespoons of superfine sugar

candied kumquat

1 cup fresh kumquats

½ cup sugar

2 tablespoons corn syrup

rice pudding: for the rice

¼ cup + 1 tablespoon jasmine rice

2 tablespoons sugar

1 cup coconut milk

½ cup whole milk

¼ teaspoon salt

rice pudding: for the custard

1 cup whole milk

½ cup heavy cream

3 egg yolks

5 tablespoons sugar, divided

8 cardamom pods

½ teaspoon vanilla extract or ½ bean

Pinch of salt (less than ¼ teaspoon)

rhubarb chips

4 thick stalks of rhubarb

½ cup super fine sugar

coconut tuile cones

4 large egg whites

¾ cup granulated sugar

½ cup all-purpose flour

½ teaspoon salt

4 ounces melted extra virgin coconut oil
(AVAILABLE IN HEALTH FOOD STORES OR WHOLE FOODS)

coconut cardamom rice pudding with rhubarb and kumquat

YIELDS FIFTEEN SERVINGS

Prepare rice: Preheat the oven to 325°F. Place rice in a strainer and rinse with cold water. Put the rice in a small ovenproof pot with two cups of cold water. Bring to a boil and immediately remove from heat. Strain the rice and discard the starchy water. Return the blanched rice back to ovenproof pot and combine with sugar, whole milk, coconut milk and salt. Bring to a boil, cover with aluminum foil or pot lid and place in oven for 30 minutes. If your pot is not oven proof, transfer the rice and liquid to a metal or glass baking dish and cover with aluminum foil. The rice is done once when it softens, expands, and has absorbed all liquids. If there is still runny milk in pot, continue to bake the rice covered for another 5 to 10 minutes, or until thickened. When rice is done, leave covered and set aside in a warm spot.

Prepare custard: While rice is baking, make the custard. Using the bottom of a small fry pan, crush the cardamom pods so they split open. In a saucepan, over medium heat, combine cardamom (pods and seeds), two tablespoons of sugar, milk, and heavy cream; bring mixture to a simmer. Once simmering, remove from heat and allow the cardamom to steep for 10 minutes. In a mixing bowl, briskly whisk together the egg yolks and the remaining 3 tablespoons sugar for 30 seconds. Slowly, using a ladle, whisk 1/3 of the hot liquid into egg mixture to warm. Gradually pour warmed egg mixture back into pot of hot milk mixture, whisking milk constantly as you pour. Do not remove the cardamom seeds. Return the pot to medium heat, continuously stirring and scraping the bottom with a rubber spatula or wooden spoon. Remove from heat once the custard thickens enough to coat the back of a spoon. Strain custard to remove the cracked cardamom pods.

Finish rice pudding: In a large bowl, gently mix cooked rice (which should still be hot) and custard together with a whisk. Scrape back into a pot and, while stirring, gently the bring rice pudding to a simmer. Remove from heat once mixture bubbles for about 10 seconds. Serve warm or chill and serve cold.

RECIPE CONTINUES ON PAGE 148

CHANTERELLE

pastry chef

Kate Zuckerman

www.chanterellenyc.com

slow roasted pineapple

½ fresh pineapple

100 grams butter

150 grams dark brown sugar

1 vanilla bean, scraped

pineapple soup

460 grams fresh pineapple juice, from ½ pineapple

5 grams lime juice

65 grams simple syrup

frozen yogurt

500 grams Greek yogurt

250 grams crème fraîche (preferably Alouette)

250 grams simple syrup

100 grams heavy cream

50 grams milk

125 grams inverted sugar

Zest of 3 lemons

20 grams fresh lemon juice

basil foam

188 grams Foam Base (recipe follows)

5 grams fresh basil leaves

Pinch of citric acid

0.44 grams xanthan gum*

2.63 grams Versa-whip powder*

foam base

40 grams sugar

3 grams each lemon and lime juice

* XANTHAN GUM IS AVAILABLE IN HEALTH FOOD STORES.
VERSA-WHIP AND XANTHAN GUM AVAILABLE AT LEPICERIE.COM

chilled pineapple soup with frozen yogurt with slow roasted pineapple with basil

YIELDS TWENTY SERVINGS

All measurements are in metric for the purposes of accuracy, conversion tables can be found online, but we don't recommend converting the measurements.

Prepare slow roasted pineapple: Preheat oven to 325°F. Cut the top, bottom and peel off of the pineapple. Cut half of the flesh into 1/2 inch dice. Reserve the core and any scraps for the soup. Put diced pineapple in baking dish with butter, brown sugar and scraped vanilla bean. Bake for about an hour, stirring every 15 minutes, until lightly caramelized. The fruit should be soft but still hold its shape. Can be prepared up to 3 days ahead.

Prepare pineapple soup: If you don't have a juicer, you can blend the fruit and strain it through a fine sieve lined with two layers of cheesecloth. Combine pineapple juice, lime juice, and simple syrup and refrigerate until ready to use. Can be made up to one day in advance.

Prepare frozen yogurt: Combine the yogurt, crème fraîche, and syrup in a large bowl; place over another bowl of ice water and set aside. In a pot, bring the cream, milk, inverted sugar, and lemon zest to a boil. Immediately strain into yogurt mixture and whisk to combine; chill; cool. Once cool, add lemon juice. If there are any lumps of yogurt, blend with a hand blender. Process in an ice cream freezer or Pacojet according to manufacturer's instructions. Should be prepared the day of serving.

Prepare basil foam: Puree the Foam Base, basil, and citric acid in a blender, and strain through a fine meshed sieve lined with damp cheesecloth. Scale 175 grams of this liquid. Puree in the xanthan gum with a hand blender; then puree in the Versa-whip. Whip the mixture with either a hand-held mixer or a stand mixer with a whisk attachment. Foam is ready when it is stiff and has the consistency of a light shaving cream. Can be made a day in advance; rewhipped before serving.

RECIPE CONTINUES ON PAGE 149

AUREOLE

pastry chef

Jennifer Yee

www.charliepalmer.com

rhubarb compote

½ cup sugar

1 cup diced rhubarb

liquid sable

½ cup powdered sugar

¾ cup flour

¼ cup almond flour

½ teaspoon salt

1 stick (½ cup) butter, cold

simple syrup

2 ½ cups sugar

2 ¾ cups water

yogurt sorbet

11 ounces Greek yogurt

½ cup Simple Syrup (recipe above)

Zest of ½ lemon

rhubarb chips

1 large stalk of rhubarb

Simple Syrup, as needed (recipe above)

tarragon chips

12 sprigs of tarragon

vanilla oil

3 vanilla beans

⅓ cup grapeseed oil

candied lemon

2 lemons

Simple Syrup as needed (recipe above)

yogurt and fruit with vanilla and tarragon

YIELDS SIX SERVINGS — ADVANCE PREPARATION REQUIRED

Prepare rhubarb compote: In a dry sauté pan, caramelize the sugar over medium to high heat. Add the rhubarb and cook until the sugar has dissolved and nearly all of the liquid is evaporated. Set aside to cool.

Prepare liquid sable: Preheat oven to 325°F. Combine the dry ingredients in a food processor and pulse to sift. Cut the butter into small pieces and add to processor. Pulse until mixture is the consistency of sand. Line a baking sheet with parchment paper and roll the dough to fit the pan in an even layer. Bake until golden brown, 10-15 minutes, stirring every 5 minutes. Cool and return to the food processor and blend until a paste is formed. Roll mixture between two pieces of parchment to 1/4 inch thick. Place on a sheet tray and freezer to set. Then, cut into 1-inch squares and refrigerate.

Prepare simple syrup: In a saucepan, bring the sugar and water to a boil, stirring to dissolve. Cool to room temperature.

Prepare yogurt sorbet: Combine the yogurt, Simple Syrup, and zest and process in an ice cream freezer according to manufacturer's instructions.

Prepare rhubarb chips: Preheat oven to 180°F. Slice the rhubarb lengthwise on a deli slicer (or mandoline) into thin sheets. Cut slices on a bias to form diamond shapes. Place in a container and cover with Simple Syrup. Place in the refrigerator overnight. The next day drain the syrup off and place the chips on a nonstick baking mat. Place in oven until dry, 6 to 8 hours or overnight.

Prepare tarragon chips: Cover a microwave safe plate with plastic wrap very tightly so that the top is a taught, flat surface. Spray the plastic wrap lightly with nonstick spray and wipe off the excess with a paper towel. Place the individual tarragon leaves on the prepared plate and microwave on medium high until dry. This usually takes between 2 and 4 minutes but may vary with different microwaves.

Prepare vanilla oil: Scrape vanilla beans into a small metal bowl with the pods. Heat oil to 250°F and pour over vanilla. Cool to room temperature.

Prepare candied lemon: Peel the lemons, making sure to trim the pith from the zest. Cut the zest into thin strips. Place in a pan with cold water to cover and bring to a boil. Drain and repeat again. Place back in pot and cover with Simple Syrup. Simmer for 30 minutes and set aside to cool.

Assembly: Place a square of the liquid sable in the center of each plate. Place a small spoon of the rhubarb compote next to it. Top the sable with a small scoop of yogurt sorbet. Place some Greek yogurt in a small squeeze bottle and pipe a small dot between the sorbet and compote. Arrange one each of the chips and a candied lemon strip on top. Place a few drops of vanilla oil on top and around the plate.

anthos

pastry chef
Zak Miller

www.anthos.com

three ring circus

phyllo ring

5 sheets phyllo dough

½ stick (4 tbls) of butter, melted

¼ cup of sugar

yogurt raspberry filling

3 sheets gelatin

1 cup cream, divided

1 cup Greek yogurt

1 tablespoon vanilla extract

2 tablespoons sugar

⅛ cup (or about 6) raspberries

mango wrap

4 sheets gelatin

1 cup mango puree

1 heaping tablespoon cornstarch

2 tablespoons simple syrup

Prepare phyllo ring: Preheat oven to 325°F. Place a sheet of phyllo dough on a parchment paper-lined baking sheet. Brush melted butter onto dough and sprinkle with sugar. Repeat process to make five layers. Place another sheet of parchment paper and then another sheet pan on top to keep the dough flat. Bake until golden, about 12 minutes. While hot, cut 10 strips of dough, approximately 7 x 1½" and wrap around a 3 x 1½" ring mold to set shape; cool and store in a dry place.

Prepare yogurt raspberry filling: Submerge the gelatin sheets in a bowl of cold water for 10 minutes; remove and squeeze out excess water. Combine half of the cream, yogurt, vanilla, and sugar in a bowl; set aside. Warm the remaining ½ cup cream and add the gelatin, stirring to dissolve. Incorporate the gelatin mix into yogurt. Fold in raspberries; rest in refrigerator for a least one hour before shaping. Transfer mixture to a piping bag fitted with a round tip.

Prepare mango wrap: Submerge the gelatin sheets in a bowl of cold water for 10 minutes; remove and squeeze out excess water. Line a sheet tray with plastic wrap as flat as possible. In a heavy-bottom pan, heat the mango puree. In a small bowl, mix the cornstarch with simple syrup; add some of hot puree and mix together. Return starch-mango mixture to pan and bring to a simmer for 3 to 4 minutes. Add the gelatin to hot mix, stirring to dissolve. Pour the hot mixture out on the lined sheet tray and spread thin (about ½ cm). Chill in the refrigerator and then slice the mango wrap into 3" thick strips. Pipe yogurt raspberry filling in a line to one side of mango wrap. Lift this side of the mango wrap and roll up and around the raspberry filling to enclose, making logs. Cut the logs into 1½" thick pieces.

To serve: Place one piece of the yogurt filled mango wrap inside the phyllo ring.

MANDARIN ORIENTAL
NEW YORK

pastry chef
Paul Nolan

www.mandarinoriental.com

chocolate macaron surprise

YIELDS **50** COOKIES

1 cup egg whites

3 ½ cups powdered sugar, divided

1 ¾ cups almond flour

½ tablespoon cocoa powder

Ganache (recipe follows)

Fondant, optional

Chocolate sauce (recipe follows)

Cocoa nibs

Pulled sugar

ganache

8 ounces chopped bittersweet chocolate

¾ cup heavy cream

chocolate sauce

6 ounces chopped bittersweet chocolate

¼ cup water

2 tablespoons granulated sugar

HARD TO FIND ITEMS AVAILABLE AT BAKING SUPPLY
SHOPS OR FROM LEPICERIE.COM

In a mixing bowl, whip egg whites while gradually adding ¼ cup powdered sugar and continue to whip to stiff peaks. Sift together remaining 3¼ cups sugar with the almond flour and cocoa powder. Gently fold the dry mixture into the egg whites until mixture falls slightly and becomes shiny. Transfer to pastry bag fitted with a small round tip.

Preheat oven to 275°F. Pipe one-inch wide cookies, about 2" apart, onto a parchment paper lined baking sheet. Let cookies sit for 15 minutes, until a light crust forms. Place another baking sheet underneath and bake for about 15 to 20 minutes, or until cooked though and the bottom of the cookie does not stick to the parchment paper. Remove from the oven, and immediately pour a little water under parchment paper to free the cookies from the paper and place on another sheet pan to cool bottom side up. Pipe ganache onto half of the upturned cookies, and place another cookie on top to make a sandwich.

If using fondant, roll through a pasta machine as thin as possible. (A metal rolling pin will also work if machine is not available.) To make the stripe pattern, cut strips of different colored fondant, stick them back together and roll through a pasta machine again. Immediately shape fondant around the cookie. Decorate plate with dabs of chocolate sauce, sprinkle of cocoa nibs and pulled sugar.

Prepare ganache: Place chocolate in medium size bowl. Heat cream in a saucepan until full boil. Pour cream over chocolate. Stir with a whisk until chocolate is melted and mixture is smooth. Cool to room temperature. Transfer to a piping bag.

Prepare chocolate sauce: Fill a small saucepot ⅓ with water, and bring to a light simmer. Place the chocolate, water, and sugar in a medium heatproof bowl and place on top of the pot (the bottom of the bowl should not touch the water). Whisk until the chocolate is melted and texture is smooth. Hold at room temperature.

THE FOUR SEASONS
RESTAURANT

executive pastry chef

Patrick Lemble

www.fourseasonsrestaurant.com

small things SWEET

custard base for bread pudding

200 grams sugar

720 grams egg yolk

1 kilogram milk

1 kilogram heavy cream

corn bread

560 grams all-purpose flour

620 grams cornmeal

48 grams baking powder

120 grams sugar

20 grams salt

450 grams butter

2 vanilla beans, scraped

8 eggs

960 grams milk

250 grams honey

250 grams maple syrup

corn bread pudding

500 grams corn bread, diced

500 grams Custard Base (recipe above)

corn tuile

90 grams freeze dried corn

510 grams water

180 grams sugar

180 grams glucose powder

2 grams salt

Dessicant, as needed

lemongrass crème anglaise

250 grams milk

250 grams cream

125 grams minced lemongrass

25 grams sugar

90 grams egg yolk

corn bread pudding with lemongrass & prune

YIELDS EIGHT SERVINGS — ADVANCE PREPARATION REQUIRED

All measurements are in metric for the purposes of accuracy, conversion tables can be found online, but we don't recommend converting the measurements.

Prepare custard base: Whisk the sugar and egg yolks together in a medium bowl. Heat the milk and cream in a saucepan to a boil; remove from heat. Slowly stream the hot cream mixture into the yolks while whisking. Transfer the mixture to a bowl set over another bowl of ice water, stirring to chill; refrigerate.

Prepare corn bread: Preheat oven to 300°F and line a baking sheet with parchment paper. In a bowl combine the flour, cornmeal, baking powder, sugar and salt. Heat the butter in a saucepot until browned; add the scraped vanilla beans and strain into a bowl. Add the remaining wet ingredients to the brown butter and whisk to combine. Fold in the dry ingredients and transfer batter to prepared baking sheet. Bake for 20 minutes, or until golden brown and cooked through. Cool to room temperature. Cut into medium dice and reserve.

Prepare corn bread pudding: Preheat oven to 300°F. Mix the corn bread and Custard Base together and pipe into 1.5-inch cylindrical flexi molds placed in a baking pan. Pour water into the baking pan to reach 2/3 the way up the flexi molds. Bake until set (about 20 minutes), then cool to room temperature. Freeze puddings, then unmold and store refrigerated in an airtight container.

Prepare corn tuile: Combine all the ingredients in a blender and puree until very smooth. Spread a paper thin layer of the puree onto 3 x 3 inch acetate squares. Place squares in a dehydrator and dehydrate at 150°F for 12 hours. Sprinkle enough dessicant to cover the bottom of a airtight container and place in the corn tuiles to store; cover.

Prepare lemongrass crème anglaise: Bring the milk and cream to a boil. Add the lemongrass and simmer for 5 minutes. Cover the infusion and infuse at room temperature for 30 minutes. Strain mixture, discarding the lemongrass and return to a boil. Whisk together the sugar and egg yolks in a bowl. Temper the lemongrass infusion into the yolks and return the mixture to a very low heat. Stir constantly until the mixture coats a spoon. Strain into a bowl set over another bowl of ice water to chill; refrigerate.

RECIPE CONTINUES ON PAGE 148

wd~50

pastry chef

Alex Stupak

www.wd-50.com

raspberry and gold joconde

YIELDS THIRTY SERVINGS

joconde biscuit

81.25 grams egg whites

20 grams sugar

43.75 grams powdered sugar

5 grams gingerbread spices

43.75 grams almond powder

12.5 grams all-purpose flour

62.5 grams eggs, whipped

10 grams butter

1 tablespoon raspberry liquor

vanilla cream cheese

125 grams cream cheese

1 cup plus 1 teaspoon sugar

20 grams mascarpone

10 grams fromage blanc

1 teaspoon of dark rum

garnish

60 fresh raspberries

30 chocolate cones*

Fresh dill

1 gold duster or a can of gold spray*

30 chocolate spoons*

Pulled sugar

Zest of 1 lime, cut into diamond shape

Toasted pumpkin seeds, crushed

*AVAILABLE AT BAKING SUPPLY SHOPS OR FROM LEPICERIE.COM

All measurements are in metric for the purposes of accuracy, conversion tables can be found online, but we don't recommend converting the measurements.

Prepare joconde biscuit: Preheat oven to 340°F. Using a whisk, whip the egg whites and sugar to a firm peaks. In the bowl of an electric mixer fitted with whisk attachment, combine icing sugar, gingerbread spices, almond powder and all-purpose flour. Add the eggs gradually in a stream. Add the butter. Fold in egg whites. Let the mix fall a little, then use a metal spatula to spread a fine layer on a silpat-lined baking sheet. Bake for 7 minutes. Cool, then cut 30 pieces to desired size.

Prepare vanilla cream cheese: In a large bowl, using a whisk, combine the cream cheese, sugar, mascarpone, fromage blanc, and dark rum to a smooth consistency; being careful not to over-whip. Immediately transfer to a piping bag, with a tip of your choice. Refrigerate until ready to use.

Assembly: Place one piece of the joconde biscuit on each plate. Pipe a small amount of the vanilla cream cheese on the biscuit, with a quartered raspberry on top. Place a chocolate cone into the back of the cut raspberry and a sprig of dill into the top; dust with the gold. Then, for each serving, stuff a whole raspberry with a little of the cream cheese filling. Prop the chocolate spoon, sprayed with the gold, on to the stuffed raspberry. Garnish the spoon with pulled sugar and a diamond shaped piece of lime zest. Finish by arranging a line of crushed pumpkin seeds on the plate.

THE RUSSIAN TEA ROOM

executive chef   chef de cuisine

Marc Taxiera   Petrous Moldovan

www.russiantearoomnyc.com

pastry

½ cup all-purpose flour

2 tablespoons cornstarch

1 teaspoon potato starch, plus extra
for dusting

2 tablespoons sugar

½ teaspoon salt

2 egg yolks

¼ cup coconut milk

¼ cup Lime Slaked Water (recipe follows)

Vegetable oil, as needed

lime slaked water

3 drops of lemon juice (with 1 qt water)

squash chantilly

¼ cup squash, steamed

2 tablespoons honey

2 tablespoons cream cheese

¼ teaspoon salt

¼ cup whipped cream

walnut cookie crust

7 ounces walnuts

2 cups butter

8 ounces sugar

7 ½ ounces brown sugar

½ teaspoon salt

2 eggs

1 teaspoon vanilla

14 ounces all-purpose flour

⅓ ounce baking powder

⅓ ounce baking soda

garnish (per serving)

⅛ teaspoon passionfruit juice with seeds

Rose candy

Maldon salt

Micro mint

passionfruit & squash cheese cups

YIELDS **16** SERVINGS — ADVANCE PREPARATION REQUIRED

Prepare pastry: In the bowl of an electric mixer fitted with a paddle attachment, mix all ingredients together until it forms a smooth ball. Remove dough from mixer; wrap it in plastic, set aside for a minimum of 2 hours at room temperature.

Fill a medium heavy-bottom pot ⅓ way full with vegetable oil and using, a candy thermometer, heat to 350°F. Roll dough on a surface lightly dusted with potato starch until dough is ¹⁄₁₆" thick. Cut dough into (16) 3-inch circles. Place pastry pieces in 1x1" fluted molds, cover with another mold and deep fry in batches until shape is formed and set. Remove the top mold and continue to fry until dough is golden brown. Remove from the oil with a spider or slotted spoon, then strain and cool on paper towels.

Prepare lime slaked water: Put 3 drops of lemon juice in a quart of water into a bowl and set aside overnight. *Chef's note*: Lime slaked water is a staple in many Asian pastry recipes, keeps the dough from getting tough, similar to using a bit of vinegar in pie dough.

Prepare squash chantilly: In a food processor, puree squash with honey, salt, and cream cheese until smooth. Transfer to a mixing bowl, fold in whipped cream and transfer chantilly to a piping bag.

Prepare walnut cookie crust: Preheat oven to 350°F. Cream butter, walnut, salt, and sugars to light and fluffy. Scrape bowl with a rubber spatula; add the egg and vanilla. Add in the flour, baking powder, and baking soda, and mix until fully incorporated. Wrap with plastic wrap and chill for at least 4 hours. Spread batter between 2 pieces of parchment until ¼" thick. Bake until brown, about 8 minutes. Cool completely. Break into smaller pieces and chop with a knife until broken into crumbs. Store in airtight container in a dry and cool area until ready to use. Keeps for about a week.

Assembly: Pipe about 1 tablespoon of squash chantilly into the pastry cup, top off with a sprinkle of passionfruit juice and seeds. Garnish with rose candy, a tiny pinch of salt and micro mint. Sit the garnished shell on top of crumbled walnut cookie crust.

chef - owner

Pichet Ong

brioche sliders with lavender gelato

lavender gelato

9 large yolks

⅔ cup sugar, divided

2 cups whole milk

2 cups heavy cream

½ teaspoon kosher salt

½ vanilla bean, scraped, seeds reserved

½ cup roughly chopped lavender sprigs

brioche sliders

¾ cup high gluten flour

2 teaspoons sugar

2 large eggs

1 teaspoon active dry yeast

1 teaspoon kosher salt

4 ounces chilled unsalted butter, cut into small pieces plus extra as needed

Coarse sugar, as needed

garnish

Lavender sprigs

Prepare lavender gelato: In a large bowl, whisk together the egg yolks and 1/3 cup of the sugar. In a large saucepan, whisk together the milk, cream, remaining 1/3 cup sugar, salt, and vanilla bean and seeds; place a bowl of ice water on the side. Bring the mixture to a full boil, and then, as soon as it begins to rise up the sides, remove the pan from the heat. Whisk about one cup hot milk mixture into the yolks, whisking to combine. Pour the egg yolk mixture back into pan. Add the chopped lavender. Transfer to a bowl and place over the ice water; let stand at room temperature for one hour Strain the cooled custard through a fine mesh sieve into a bowl. Cover bowl and refrigerate the custard overnight. Freeze the custard in an ice cream maker, following the manufacturer's directions.

Prepare brioche sliders: In the bowl of an electric mixer fitted with a dough hook, mix together the flour and sugar. Whisk eggs and yeast together over a pot of simmering water until they are warm to the touch. Add the eggs to the flour mixture and mix on medium speed until the dough comes together in a ball. Add the salt. Still on medium speed, add the butter quickly, piece by piece. Continue mixing until the dough is shiny and makes a slapping sound. Transfer to a large buttered bowl, cover with plastic wrap and let the dough double. Punch down the dough and refrigerate overnight. Preheat the oven to 375°F. Weigh the chilled dough out to 12 gram pieces, and shape with your palm into balls, similar to a dinner roll. Space them evenly on a baking sheet. Cover with plastic wrap and let them rise until doubled. Remove plastic and brush with melted butter then sprinkle with coarse sugar. Bake sliders for about 6 minutes, until golden brown. Remove the pan from oven and let cool. Slice buns in half, like a hamburger bun. Brush them with soft butter and toast the cut side on a griddle or hot sauté pan.

Assembly: Sandwich a scoop of gelato or sorbetto in each bun. Serve immediately. Garnish with lavender sprigs.

LOCANDA VERDE

pastry chef

Karen DeMasco

www.locandaverdenyc.com

macerated oranges
with stuffed dates and pistachios

YIELDS SIX SERVINGS

3 oranges, peeled

2 tablespoons grappa

2 tablespoons honey

¾ cup mascarpone cheese

1½ tablespoons sugar

¼ teaspoon cinnamon

¼ teaspoon instant espresso

2 ounces bittersweet chocolate, chopped

12 Medjool dates

1 cup salted pistachio nuts, in shell

Section oranges by cutting away the skin, then slice each section from the membrane. Place in a medium-size serving bowl. Stir in the grappa and honey. Cover and refrigerate until ready to use. In another bowl, mix together the mascarpone, sugar, cinnamon, and espresso until well combined. Stir in the chocolate and set aside. Cut a lengthwise slit in each of the dates and remove pit. Fill each date with 3/4 teaspoon of the cheese mixture. For each serving, plate 2 stuffed dates and a few pistachio nuts alongside a small bowl of chilled oranges.

small things SWEET

Lucinda Scala Quinn

chef - author

"Lucinda's Rustic Italian Kitchen"

dark chocolate earl grey cream
(yield: approximately 500g)

10 grams Earl Grey tea

140 grams whole milk

2 sheets gelatin

10 grams glucose

180 grams dark chocolate, chopped

155 grams heavy cream (36% fat)

milk chocolate-anise cream
[yield: approximately 500g]

3 sheets gelatin

125 grams whole milk

7 grams star anise

Zest of ½ orange

10 grams glucose

195 grams milk chocolate, chopped

170 grams heavy cream (36% fat)

caramelized white chocolate cream
(yield: approximately 480g)

3 sheets gelatin

170 grams caramelized white chocolate

10 grams glucose

125 grams whole milk

175 grams heavy cream (36% fat)

a study in chocolate and citrus

YIELDS 50 SERVINGS — ADVANCE PREPARATION REQUIRED

All measurements are in metric for the purposes of accuracy, conversion tables can be found online, but we don't recommend converting the measurements.
Prepare dark chocolate earl grey cream: Infuse the tea in the milk, refrigerated, for 12 hours. Strain and discard the tea. Add more milk as necessary to yield 140g. Submerge the gelatin sheets in a bowl of cold water for 10 minutes; remove and squeeze out excess water. Combine milk, and glucose in a medium saucepot and bring to a boil. Remove from heat and stir in the gelatin until dissolved. Whisk in the dark chocolate to melt and combine. Add the cream and emulsify for a few minutes with a Immersion blender. Transfer to a container and chill, allowing to crystallize (set), or dispense into dark chocolate shells.

Prepare milk chocolate-anise cream: Submerge the gelatin sheets in a bowl of cold water for 10 minutes; remove and squeeze out excess water. Combine milk, star anise, orange zest, and glucose in a saucepot; bring to a boil. Remove from the heat, cover and infuse for 30 minutes. Strain and return the milk to a simmer. Stir in the gelatin until dissolved. Remove from heat and slowly add in the milk chocolate until melted and smooth. Add the cream and emulsify for a few minutes with a hand immersion blender. Transfer to a container and chill, allowing to crystallize (or dispense into milk chocolate shells).

Prepare caramelized white chocolate cream: Submerge the gelatin sheets in a bowl of cold water for 10 minutes; remove and squeeze out excess water. Place the white chocolate in a heatproof bowl over a pot of simmering water (being sure that the bottom of the bowl does not touch the water), and heat until warm, stirring occasionally to form a smooth slightly thickened liquid. Add the glucose. Bring the milk to a boil and stir in the gelatin to dissolve. Remove from heat and slowly incorporate into the white chocolate. Add cream and emulsify for a few minutes with a immersion blender. Transfer to a container and chill, allowing to crystallize, (or dispense into white chocolate shells).

RECIPE CONTINUES ON PAGE 150

Le Bernardin

executive pastry chef

Michael Laiskonis

www.le-bernardin.com

milk chocolate rose macaron

YIELDS 25 COOKIES — ADVANCE PREPARATION REQUIRED

15 ounces 40% chocolate, chopped (preferably Valrhona's Jivara)

1¼ cups heavy cream

1 tablespoon glucose syrup

1 teaspoon rose water

rose macaron

1½ cups almond flour

1½ cups powdered sugar

½ cup egg whites, divided

½ teaspoon egg white powder

¾ cup granulated sugar

Pinch of cream of tartar

½ tablespoon ground dried rose petals

garnish

Dried rose petals

Prepare rose ganache: Place the chocolate in a heatproof bowl. In a saucepan, heat the heavy cream and glucose to just under a boil. Pour cream over chocolate and let melt untouched for two minutes. Stir cream into chocolate slowly making a smooth, shiny emulsion. Stir in rose water. Place plastic wrap directly on the surface of the ganache to avoid forming a skin. Cool to room temperature and thickened. Transfer to a piping bag fitted with a number 802 round tip.

Prepare rose macaron: Blend the almond flour with the powdered sugar in food processor for 30 seconds. Drizzle in 1/4 cup egg whites and blend to make a smooth wet paste; transfer to large mixing bowl. Cover with a wet towel.

Whisk together the remaining 1/4 cup egg whites and egg white powder in a 5 quart KitchenAid bowl or stand mixer. Place the granulated sugar in a small copper pot. Use your hand to mix a small amount of water into the sugar, making a slurry. Make sure there are no sugar crystals stuck to the side of the pot. Cover pot and place over medium heat. Boil, remove lid and add cream of tartar. Do not stir. Bring sugar mixture to 118°C (244.4°F). When sugar is at 115°C (239°F) whip egg white mixture to soft peaks. At 118°C slowly stream the hot sugar syrup down the side of mixer bowl while whipping. Continue whipping to stiff peaks.

Preheat oven to 265°F and position a rack in the center. Remove the wet towel from almond-sugar paste and sprinkle ground rose petals on top. Fold meringue into the sugar/almond paste mixture with a rubber spatula; until smooth and well combined. Continue folding until mixture loosens, the crests and lines from folding should disappear very slowly. Be careful not to over fold the batter; the cookies will be too flat. Immediately transfer batter to a piping bag fitted with a number 802 round tip. Pipe silver-dollar sized rounds onto a silpat covered sheet pan. Place a dried rose petal on top of half of the cookies. Dry at room temperature until a thin crust is formed but the cookie is still soft in the center, about 30 minutes to an hour depending on the humidity in the air. Bake for 12 to 15 minutes, rotating pan 180 degrees half way through. Cool completely.

To assemble: Pipe a dot of rose ganache onto the flat bottom of the cookies without rose petals, and place the cookie with the rose petal flat side down on top to make a sandwich. Place on a tray and wrap tray gently with plastic wrap. Refrigerate overnight. Unwrap and allow cookies to come to room temperature. Garnish each cookie with a rose petal.

small things SWEET

ELEVEN MADISON PARK

executive pastry chef

Angela Pinkerton

www.elevenmadisonpark.com

sable dough

1½ cups soft butter

¾ cup powdered sugar

15 ounces all-purpose flour

2 large eggs

Zest of 1 lemon

½ teaspoon salt

vanilla bean cheesecake

4¼ cups cream cheese

1½ cups mascarpone

2 cups sugar

2 vanilla beans, split and scraped

5 eggs

¾ cup heavy cream

sponge cake

8 large eggs

1 cup all-purpose flour

1 cup granulated sugar

tres leches soak

1½ cups whole milk

1 cup evaporated milk

1 cup condensed milk

raspberry filling

½ cup sugar

2 tablespoons apple pectin

1¼ cups raspberry puree

1 pint fresh raspberries

white chocolate mousse

2 sheets gelatin

1 large egg

2 egg yolks

8 ounces white chocolate

2 egg whites

1¼ cups heavy cream

raspberry tres leches cheesecake

YIELDS ABOUT 200 BITE-SIZE PIECES — ADVANCE PREPARATION REQUIRED

Prepare sable dough: In the bowl of an electric mixer fitted with a paddle attachment, combine the soft butter and sugar to just to incorporate. Add lemon zest. Add eggs one at the time mixing to combine in-between each addition. Add flour and salt and mix just to combine, being sure not to over mix. Wrap dough with plastic wrap overnight.

Preheat oven to 325°F and position a rack in the center. Roll the dough on a well-floured surface until dough is 1/4 inch thick. Let rest at least 2 hours. Transfer to a 13-inch wide by 18-inch long by 3/4-inch high baking pan, pressing an even layer of dough over bottom and up sides of pan. Chill for 45 minutes. Lightly prick entire shell with a fork. Bake until sides are set and edges are golden, about 15 minutes. Transfer pan to a rack to cool.

Prepare vanilla bean cheesecake: Preheat oven to 120°F. Beat together cream cheese, mascarpone and sugar in a bowl of an electric mixer fitted with paddle attachment on medium speed until smooth. Reduce speed to low and scrape in seeds from vanilla beans. Add eggs one at a time and stir in heavy cream until incorporated. Pour filling into cooled sable dough crust. Bake until filling is set 1½ inches from edge but center is wobbly, 45 to 50 minutes (filling will continue to set as it cools) transfer cake pan to a rack and immediately run a knife around edge. Cool completely, 2 to 3 hours. Refrigerate until ready to use.

Prepare sponge cake: Preheat oven to 325°F and position a rack in the center. In an electric mixer, whisk eggs and sugar until it doubles in size, transfer mix to a larger mixing bowl and gradually fold in flour. Pour mix onto a parchment paper lined 13 x 18 x 1-inch baking pan and bake for about 10 minutes, rotate pan 180° and bake for an additional 3 minutes, until lightly golden. Transfer to a rack to cool.

Prepare tres leches soak: In a heavy saucepan, bring whole and evaporated milk to boil, remove from heat, add condensed milk and whisk to incorporate. Strain and transfer the liquid to a bowl or container set over another bowl of ice water, and stir occasionally until well chilled. Set aside.

RECIPE CONTINUES ON PAGE 149

DOS CAMINOS

executive pastry chef

Hugo Reyes

www.brguestrestaurants.com

chocolate whiskey sponge

300 grams sugar

21 grams agar-agar

750 grams whole milk

600 grams dark chocolate, preferably
Valrhona Guanaja, melted

327 grams whiskey

Dark chocolate spray

frozen spiced chocolate powder

300 grams water

30 grams cocoa powder

30 grams sugar

100 grams heavy cream

75 grams dark chocolate, 70%

3 grams Pepper Mix (recipe follows)

pepper mix

20 grams pink peppercorns

10 grams black peppercorns

10 grams sichuan peppercorns

purple corn puff

2000 grams water

425 grams purple corn cobs, dried

100 grams sugar

500 grams purple corn syrup

5 grams Methocel F-50

0.5 grams xanthan gum

garnish

Blackberries, halved

Walnuts, toasted, grated

chocolate whiskey sponge, pepper powder, purple corn puff

YIELDS 30 TO 33 SERVINGS — ADVANCE PREPARATION REQUIRED

All measurements are in metric for the purposes of accuracy, conversion tables can be found online, but we don't recommend converting the measurements.

Prepare chocolate whiskey sponge: Combine the sugar and agar and mix well. Fill blender with milk and slowly pour agar-agar and sugar into milk while blender is on. Transfer to a pot and bring to a boil while whisking periodically. Reduce to a simmer and continue cooking for 5 minutes. Whisk in melted chocolate. Add whiskey and mix well. Pour chocolate gel into 3 20-ounce soda bottles. Squeeze bottle to remove excess air then carbonate at 50 psi. Shake vigorously. Cool the mix slightly under cold water, continue to shake. Release pressure from bottle carefully and pour chocolate gel into a deep container. Place container in Cryovac machine. Cryovac chocolate gel. Turn off the machine when gel has risen up and is at full volume. (Do not let it boil or you will lose your air). Leave in machine to set, about 30 minutes. Remove gel from pan and cut into 1-inch cubes. Tear cubes in half along a diagonal to resemble rocks.

Prepare frozen spiced chocolate powder: Bring the water to a simmer. Whisk in cocoa powder and sugar and bring to a boil. Whisk in the cream and chocolate, strain and then cool. Pour into Pacojet container, add Pepper Mix and blend with an immersion blender. Freeze. Process two portions on Pacojet, stop machine and remove layer of powder. Repeat until entire container is processed. Store in freezer.

Prepare purple corn puff: Bring the water and corn to a boil and simmer for an hour. Remove husks and strain liquid. Reserve purple corn syrup in refrigerator. Preheat oven to 200°F. Place syrup in a bowl of a stand mixer fitted with whisk attachment. Whisk powders together and slowly add to syrup. Whip to a stiff peak, or until a firm foam forms, scraping down sides of bowl often to avoid lumps. Gently transfer the foam to a Silpat-lined sheet pan and spread slightly. Bake for one hour and then transfer to a hot box or dehydrator overnight. Store in dehydrator or an airtight container.

Assembly: For each serving, place a small amount of frozen spiced chocolate powder in the bottom of bowl. Arrange two pieces of the chocolate whiskey sponge and two pieces or purple corn puff. Garnish with blackberries and walnuts.

NOTE: HARD TO FIND ITEMS AVAILABLE AT BAKING SUPPLY SHOPS OR ONLINE FROM LEPICERIE.COM OR SIMILAR SITES.

executive pastry chef

Johnny Iuzzini

www.jean-georges.com

soft ganache

750 grams chocolate, 70%, chopped

795 grams heavy cream

180 grams sugar

900 grams water

5 grams carrageenan

tahini ice cream

4000 grams milk

2000 grams heavy cream

300 grams glucose

300 grams trimoline

1300 grams sugar

1320 grams yolks

800 grams tahini paste

20 grams salt

kuro goma soil

300 grams black sesame paste

100 grams tapioca maltodextrin

400 grams powdered sugar

kuro goma glaze

300 grams black sesame paste

70 grams sugar

100 grams whole milk, warm

2 grams salt

pâte choux puffs

110 grams butter

240 grams milk

140 grams flour

10 grams sugar

10 grams salt

5 eggs

soft chocolate ganache, black sesame, toasted sesame ice cream

YIELDS SIX SERVINGS — ADVANCE PREPARATION REQUIRED

All measurements are in metric for the purposes of accuracy, conversion tables can be found on line, but we don't recommend converting the measurements.

Prepare ganache: Line two 13 x 18" pans with plastic wrap, ensuring no wrinkles. Place chocolate in a heat proof bowl. In a medium pot, bring cream and sugar to a boil. Pour over chocolate and mix to create a smooth emulsified ganache. In a separate container, blend the water and carrageenan. When fully combined, blend into the chocolate mixture with a hand held blender. Place all ingredients back in medium pot and cook, over medium heat until mixture reaches a boil, stirring constantly. Immediately pour onto sheet tray, cool, then cut into (60) 1 x 5 cm rectangles, three per plate.

Prepare ice cream: Bring milk, cream, glucose, trimoline, and sugar to a boil. Temper in the egg yolks, and then cook until mixture coats the back of a spoon (about 170°F). While still warm, with a hand blender, emulsify the tahini and salt into base. Spin ice cream in machine as recommended by manufacturer.

Prepare kuro goma soil: Combine all ingredients in very dry food processor. Process until ingredients come together and resemble fine cornmeal. Reserve for plating.

Prepare glaze: Combine all ingredients in food processor. Process until emulsified and smooth. Remove from the bowl and reserve, chilled.

Prepare pâte choux puffs: Preheat oven to 325°F. Bring butter and milk to a boil in medium pot. Add flour, sugar, and salt and cook over medium heat, constantly stirring with a wooden spoon, until a smooth, tight ball is formed. Remove from heat and beat eggs in, one at a time, until glossy batter is formed. Transfer to a piping bag fitted with a round tip and pipe dots the size of a pencil eraser onto a 13 x 18" sheet tray. Bake until golden.

To plate: Using a brush, make one stroke of kuro goma glaze across the center of each plate; drag a fork through the glaze to creating a design. Stagger 3 soft ganache rectangles towards the back of the band separate, with a thin strip of chocolate behind each rectangle. Place some kuro goma soil on plates topped with a quenelle of ice cream. Garnish the ganache as well as the plate with pâte choux puffs.

NOTE: HARD TO FIND ITEMS AVAILABLE AT BAKING SUPPLY SHOPS OR ONLINE FROM LEPICERIE.COM OR SIMILAR SITES.

morimoto

pastry chef
Daniel Skurnick
www.morimotonyc.com

lemon pound cake (yields 1 small loaf)

1 stick plus 1½ tablespoons butter

1⅓ cups sugar

1 teaspoon lemon zest

¾ cup eggs (about 4 large eggs)

1½ cups plus 1 tablespoon all-purpose flour

¼ tablespoon baking soda

⅛ tablespoon baking powder

⅛ tablespoon salt

Pinch of poppy seeds

½ cup plus 3 tablespoons buttermilk

6 tablespoons lemon juice

⅛ cup sour cream

prosecco and elderflower dressing

⅓ cup sugar

2 tablespoons pectin

2 cups Prosecco sparkling wine, divided

1 vanilla bean, split and scraped

6 tablespoons St. Germain Elderflower

Very fine zest of ½ lime

tarragon yogurt mousseline

1 cup heavy cream

2 tablespoons honey

2 stems fresh tarragon

2½ sheets gelatin

1 cup powdered sugar

2 cups Greek yogurt

candied lemon zest

Peel of 1 lemon

2 cups sugar

garnish

Pink grapefruit segments

Strawberries, diced

8 fresh tarragon sprigs

pink grapefruit, tarragon yogurt mousseline and lemon cake croutons

YIELDS EIGHT SERVINGS — ADVANCE PREPARATION REQUIRED

Prepare lemon pound cake: Preheat oven to 325°F and position a rack in the center. Cream the butter, sugar, and lemon zest until smooth and light in color. Add eggs one by one, beating well after each addition, scraping bowl often. In a mixing bowl, combine the flour, baking soda, baking powder, salt and poppy seeds. Add half the mixed dry ingredients to the egg mixture, mixing just to incorporate. Add buttermilk and mix just until combined. Add the remaining dry mixture; just to incorporate. Add the lemon juice and sour cream and mix just until combined. Transfer to a small greased and floured loaf pan. Bake for approximately 40 minutes until a toothpick inserted in the center comes out clean. Chill.

Prepare dressing: Mix sugar and pectin together. In a small pot, add the sugar mixture to 1 cup of sparkling wine and vanilla bean. Bring to a boil, whisking constantly. Remove from heat and strain through a fine mesh sieve. Add the remaining sparkling wine, the liqueur, and lime zest. Chill.

Prepare tarragon yogurt mousseline: In a small pot, bring the heavy cream and honey to a boil. Remove from heat. Add tarragon, cover and steep at room temperature for 15 to 20 minutes. Chill overnight. The following day, submerge gelatin sheets in a bowl of cold water for 10 minutes; remove and squeeze out excess water. Remove tarragon stems from cream and whip to soft peaks. Set aside. In a mixing bowl, whisk together powered sugar and yogurt. Transfer gelatin in a heatproof bowl and place on top of a pot of simmering water (without touching the water); stir to dissolve. Whisk into yogurt mixture. Fold in whipped cream. Chill to set several hours.

Prepare candied lemon zest: Zest lemon peels into strips, being careful to remove the bitter white pith with a knife. In a small pot, combine peels with 2 cups of cold water. Bring to a boil and drain off the water. Repeat process 2 more times. Combine peels with 2 cups of sugar and 1 cup of cold water. Bring to a boil and simmer for approximately 10 minutes until peels have turned translucent. Chill and reserve in the syrup.

To serve: Preheat oven to 350°F. Slice the pound cake into (16) 1½ inch squares and toast in oven until golden brown. For each serving, arrange 3 pink grapefruit segments in a triangle on a plate, drizzle liberally with the Prosecco and Elderflower dressing. Sprinkle a spoonful of the small-diced strawberries around segments. Stagger two pieces of toasted pound cake on top of the segments. Top with a dollop of tarragon yogurt mousseline. Garnish with a couple pieces of candied lemon zest and a sprig of fresh tarragon.

QUALITY MEATS

executive pastry chef

Cory Colton

www.qualitymeatsnyc.com

triple citrus semifreddo

1 ¾ cups heavy cream

1 ¼ cup sugar

7 egg yolks

¼ cup Meyer lemon juice

¼ cup blood orange juice

¼ cup pink grapefruit juice

swiss meringue

2 egg whites

¼ cup sugar

ginger bomboloni

1 ounce fresh yeast

1½ tablespoons milk

2 egg yolks

3 tablespoons water

¾ cup plus 1 tablespoon all-purpose flour

2 tablespoons plus ¼ cup sugar, divided

Pinch of salt

2 tablespoons cold and cubed butter

1 teaspoon ground ginger

Canola oil, as needed

red currant sauce

½ cup red currant puree (preferably Ravifruit brand, available at lepicerie.com)

2 tablespoons sugar

Juice of ½ lemon

triple citrus "baked alaska"

YIELDS SIX TO EIGHT SERVINGS — ADVANCE PREPARATION REQUIRED

Prepare semifreddo: Whip the heavy cream to medium peaks and set aside. In a small pot, combine the sugar with enough water to cover and bring to a boil. Whip the egg yolks in a standing mixer until fluffy and slowly pour in the hot sugar liquid, whipping until the bowl is cool to the touch. Fold in the whipped cream. Separate the mousse into three separate bowls, pour one type of juice into each, and fold until they are thoroughly mixed. Spread one layer at a time according to your preference into a 10-inch cake pan and freeze overnight before cutting into desired bite-sized shapes; keep frozen.

Prepare meringue: Combine the egg whites and sugar in a stainless steel mixing bowl and place on top of a pot of simmering water (without letting the bowl touch the water). Cook, whisking until the sugar is dissolved. Whip the mixture until it reaches medium peaks. Transfer to a piping bag fitted with a star tip. When ready to serve, pipe stars onto the top of each semifreddo. Using a torch, burn the meringue to a golden brown color.

Prepare ginger bomboloni: Combine the yeast, milk, egg yolks, and water in the bowl of an electric mixer fitted with a paddle attachment and let sit for several minutes at room temperature to activate the yeast. Combine the flour and 2 tablespoons of sugar, and work into the wet ingredients, kneading until the dough comes together. Work in the butter and salt and set aside to rise for at least an hour until the dough doubles in size. Roll the dough on a lightly floured surface until 1/2 inch thick and cut into desired shapes. When ready to serve, deep fry in 350°F oil until golden brown. Remove with a slotted spoon and drain on a paper towel lined plate. While warm, dredge in a mixture of the remaining 1/4 cup sugar and ginger.

Prepare red currant sauce: Combine red currant puree, sugar and lemon juice in a saucepan;simmer until sugar is dissolved. Refrigerate to cool.

To serve: Drizzle red currant sauce on each plate in a swirl pattern. Place one of the semifreddo topped with meringue in the center, with one or two warm ginger bombolonis alongside. (Optional) Finish with a few sprigs of thyme, candied sliced almonds, and some citrus segments, if desired.

Olana

pastry chef

Katie Rosenhouse

www.olananyc.com

kaffir lime infused mango, lime almond dacquoise, mango tuile

YIELDS 50 SERVINGS — ADVANCE PREPARATION REQUIRED

lime almond dacquoise

(for 1 kilo of batter)

336 grams egg whites

112 grams sugar

247 grams almond flour

291 grams powdered sugar

14 grams fresh lime zest

mango tuile

50 grams mango puree

50 grams neutral glaze

basil seed infusion

125 grams water

38 grams sugar

4 grams Thai basil

6 grams basil seeds

garnish

2 mangos, peeled and diced ¼ inch

1 ounce micro basil

All measurements are in metric for the purposes of accuracy, conversion tables can be found online, but we don't recommend converting the measurements.

Prepare lime almond dacquoise: Preheat oven to 350°F and place a rack in the center. With a stand mixer fitted with a whisk attachment, whip the egg whites and sugar to medium peak. Sift together the almond flour and powdered sugar and slowly and slowly add into egg whites, while whisking. Add lime zest. Spread the batter onto a 13 x 18 x 1" rimmed baking tray and bake for approximately 12 minutes, or until a toothpick inserted in the center comes out clean. Cool at room temperature and cut into one-inch squares. Store covered in the refrigerator for up to one week.

Prepare mango tuile: Preheat oven to 285°F. Mix the puree with the glaze in a small saucepot and bring to a boil. Simmer to reduce by half. Chill mixture in the refrigerator overnight. Spread thin strips onto a silpat lined baking sheet and bake for 10 minutes. While still warm, cut one-inch strips out of the batter and mold half of the strip around a 4cm ring (resulting in the shape of a number 6). Cool to room temperature.

Prepare basil seed infusion: Boil the water and sugar in a small saucepot, remove from the heat and add Thai basil. Cover and infuse at room temperature for 20 minutes. Strain through a fine meshed sieve and chill the liquid. Combine with the basil seeds. Store in the refrigerator for up to one week.

To finish: Place a one-inch square of lime dacquoise inside of a mango tuile so that it stands up straight, Top each dacquoise with three mango dices and garnish with basil seeds and a sprig of micro basil.

DANIEL

pastry chef

Dominique Ansel

www.danielnyc.com

poached figs with lemon bavaroise cigarettes

YIELDS EIGHT SERVINGS

red wine vuile

444 grams red wine

296 grams sugar

148 grams butter, softened

111 grams all purpose flour

lemon bavaroise

272 grams lemon juice

528 grams heavy cream, divided

80 grams egg yolks

80 grams sugar

2 sheets gelatin

poached figs (not shown in photo)

16 large ripe figs

435 grams red wine

217 grams black currant puree,
preferably Boiron brand purees

217 grams fig puree

130 grams sugar

All measurements are in metric for the purposes of accuracy, conversion tables can be found online, but we don't recommend converting the measurements.

Prepare lemon bavaroise cigarettes: Reduce the red wine by 1/3, and re-scale to 148 grams. Preheat oven to 325°F. Whisk together in a medium bowl the butter with the sugar and flour. Slowly stream in the wine to fully combine. Spread the batter into a paper-thin layer onto a silpat-lined baking sheet and bake for approximately 10 minutes, or until lightly golden (you may need to do this in batches). Slide the silpat from the tray onto a cutting board, lay a piece of parchment paper on top, and flip the batter over onto parchment paper. Cut the tuile batter into 3 x 4" rectangles. While still warm but not too hot to touch, lift a rectangle from the silpat with a small offset spatula and mold it into a tube by wrapping it around the handle of a wooden spoon. Repeat the process to make 16 tubes. If the batter becomes too cold and brittle, flash it in the oven to warm through and continue.

Prepare lemon bavaroise: Soak the gelatin sheets in cold water for 10 minutes. Bring 48 grams of the heavy cream to a simmer in a small pot. Whisk together yolks and sugar in a bowl. Slowly whisk in the hot cream. Return to the pot, and cook on a low heat, whisking until thickened, making an anglaise sauce. Strain the gelatin, and add to the anglaise and mix until dissolved. Cool to 100°F. Whip the remaining cream to medium peak. Fold the anglaise gently into the whipped cream. Keep chilled until ready to use.

Prepare poched figs: Preheat oven to 350°F. Whisk together the red wine, both purees, and sugar in a bowl. Slice the figs in half lengthwise and place in a 9 x 9" baking pan. Reserve 1/2 cup of the sauce, and pour the rest over the figs. Cover the pan with foil and bake for 10 minutes. Stir the figs, return the foil, and bake for another 10 minutes; the figs should be tender but not too soft. Cool the figs to room temperature.

To assemble: Transfer the lemon bavaroise to a pastry bag fitted with a Bismark Tip and gently pipe into the red wine tuiles. Serve two tuiles and four fig halves per plate; garnish with the reserved 1/2 cup of fig sauce.

CAFÉ BOULUD

NEW YORK   •   PALM BEACH

pastry chef

Raphael Haasz

www.danielnyc.com

ricotta filling

1 quart whole milk

1½ cups semolina flour

2 egg yolks

1½ cups sugar

1½ cups fresh ewe's milk ricotta, drained

1 teaspoon Saigon cinnamon

Pinch of salt

2 teaspoons candied kumquat pieces, roughly chopped (or buy candied orange)

sfogliatelle dough

7 cups OO flour (or all-purpose flour)

1½ cups water

1 tablespoon honey

Pinch of salt

1 pound container lardo, room temperature

blood orange sorbet

1 quart fresh squeezed blood orange juice

Pinch of malic acid

Pinch of salt

Juice of one each lemon and lime

2 cups sorbet base syrup
(1 c. water, 1 c. sugar, ¼ c. dextrose)

blood orange juice reduction

1 cup fresh squeezed blood orange juice

Pinch of sugar

Malic acid

garnish

Citrus marigold flowers

Chocolate mint

sfogliatelle napoletane
with torn herbs and blood orange

YIELDS 15 SERVINGS — ADVANCE PREPARATION REQUIRED

Prepare ricotta filling: In a small saucepot, bring the milk and semolina to a boil, stirring with a wooden spoon until a pate forms; remove from heat. Combine egg yolk and sugar in a bowl. Gradually add a few spoonfuls of semolina mix to the yolk mixture, stir to warm (being careful not to curdle the egg). Return tempered egg mixture to saucepot of semolina mixture and stir to combine. Add the ricotta, cinnamon, and salt. Remove from heat and cool to room temperature. Add the kumquat pieces and transfer to a pastry bag. Chill until ready to use.

Prepare dough: In the bowl of a standing electric mixer fitted with the hook attachment, combine the flour, water, honey and salt. Mix starting on low speed, then mix on medium speed until a dough forms. Remove dough from mixer; wrap in plastic and refrigerate for 2 hours. Roll the dough through a pasta machine as thin as possible. Lay a flat layer of dough on a floured tray. Generously brush dough with tempered lardo. Roll dough, jelly roll style into a tube, creating many layers. Repeat with remaining dough and lardo until finished. Refrigerate overnight.

Cut quarter sized pieces of dough. Wrap each piece around your thumb to form a cone shape, accentuating layers of dough. Pipe ricotta filling into the center of the cones and arrange onto a parchment paper lined baking sheet approximately 1 inch apart. Brush tops with lardo. Bake until golden brown, about 15 minutes. Continue to bake in batches until dough and filling is finished. Serve warm.

Prepare sorbet: Combine all ingredients, taste for acidity (it should taste more acidic than sweet). Chill overnight. Process in an ice cream freezer according to the manufacturer's instructions for a smooth and creamy consistency.

Prepare blood orange juice reduction: Place the blood orange juice and sugar in a small saucepot and simmer until reduced by 2/3. Adjust with malic acid to add a hint of acidity; chill. The reduction should be thick and syrupy at refrigerator temperature.

To serve: For each serving, brush the plate with the blood orange juice reduction. Place a rustic shaped scoop of sorbet on the back edge of the reduction. Lean a Sfogliatelle Napoletane on the sorbet. Garnish with citrus marigold flowers and chocolate mint.

Chef's note: Sfogliatelle technique thanks to Peter Pastan, 2Amys, Washington DC.

pastry chef
Brooks Headley

www.delposto.com

½ cup sugar

2 tablespoons water

3 egg yolks

10 ounces Humboldt fog cheese,
passed through a fine meshed sieve

3 ounces crème fraîche

Finely grated zest of 2 oranges

Finely grated zest of 2 lemons

1 vanilla bean, scraped

2 cups heavy cream, whipped

cabernet reduction

2 cups Cabernet Sauvignon

½ cup sugar

½ vanilla bean

Zest of ½ orange and ½ lemon, in strips

1 cinnamon stick

2 bay leaves

½ teaspoon freshly grated nutmeg

honey crisps (yields about 12 crisps)

½ cup (1 stick) butter

½ cup honey

⅓ cup sugar

1 cup flour

½ teaspoon black pepper

garnish

8-10 black figs, cut into quarters
or eights, depending on their size

¼ cup chopped toasted walnuts

small things SWEET

humboldt fog mousse with honey crisps and figs in a cabernet reduction

YIELDS SIX SERVINGS

Prepare mousse: Combine the sugar and water in a saucepot and simmer to reach 235° to 240°F (soft ball stage). Meanwhile, whip the egg yolks in a stand mixer until very pale and thick. Pour syrup down side of bowl into the whipping yolks. Whip until mixture is at room temperature. In a separate bowl, combine Humboldt fog and crème fraîche with zests and vanilla seeds. Fold cooled yolks into cheese mixture. Fold in whipped cream; chill.

Prepare reduction: Combine all ingredients in a medium sized saucepot and reduce to 1/4 cup. Strain through a fine meshed sieve and keep at room temperature.

Prepare honey crisps: Preheat oven to 325°F and place a rack in the center. Melt butter in a small saucepan. Whisk in the honey and sugar. Bring to a simmer. Remove pan from heat and whisk in pepper and flour. Drop by level teaspoonfuls on to a silpat. Batter will spread - leave a lot of space between crisps. Bake until batter spreads and turns golden brown, about 12 minutes. Let cool on the silpat, then remove with an offset spatula.

Assembly: Toss figs in the cabernet reduction. Place one honey crisp on each plate. Place a small scoop of mousse on each crisp, then top with some of the fig mixture, drizzling the cabernet reduction on top. Then top with another crisp. Top that crisp with a little more mousse and toasted walnuts. Garnish plates with some figs and cabernet reduction. Serve immediately.

brooklyn
Bunnery

chef - owner

Vicki Wells

chocolate cake

2 cups plus 2 tablespoons sugar

¾ cup all-purpose flour

¾ cup plus 2 tablespoons cocoa powder,
preferably Valrhona

1½ teaspoons baking powder

1½ teaspoons baking soda

1½ teaspoons salt

2 eggs

1 cup whole milk

½ cup vegetable oil

2½ teaspoons vanilla extract

¾ cup plus 2 tablespoons boiling water

peanut dacquoise

2 egg whites, room temperature

1 tablespoon sugar

⅓ cup almond flour

½ cup powdered sugar

½ cup unsalted peanuts, coarsely chopped

peanut butter crunch

1 cup Skippy creamy peanut butter

1½ tablespoons unsalted butter

3 ounces milk chocolate, chopped

¾ cup Rice Krispies or cornflakes, crushed

ganache

1 pound milk chocolate, chopped

1½ cups heavy cream

whipped milk chocolate ganache

4 ounces milk chocolate, chopped

8 ounces heavy cream

garnish

Almonds

Chocolate strips

chocolate peanut butter crunch cake

YIELDS 12 TO 16 SERVINGS — ADVANCE PREPARATION REQUIRED

Prepare chocolate cake: Preheat oven to 350°F and place a rack in the center. Sift together the sugar, flour, cocoa powder, baking powder, baking soda, and salt. In a separate bowl, whisk together the eggs, milk, oil, and vanilla. Combine the wet ingredients into the dry, whisking until combined. Add the boiling water and stir to combine well. (The batter is very thin, about the consistency of heavy cream). Pour the batter into a 9 x 13" pan that has been sprayed with nonstick spray. Bake for 30 to 40 minutes (the cake should spring back when touched in the middle). Remove and cool the cake.

Prepare peanut dacquoise: Preheat oven to 325°F. Trace a 9 x 13" rectangle onto a sheet of parchment paper. Turn the paper over onto a baking sheet. Whip egg whites to soft peaks, gradually begin adding granulated sugar and continue whipping until stiff and shiny. Sift the almond flour and powdered sugar over the whipped egg whites; fold together. Spread mixture evenly over the 9 x 13" rectangle. Sprinkle with the chopped peanuts and bake until lightly browned all over, about 15 minutes.

Prepare peanut butter crunch: Combine peanut butter, butter, and chocolate in a large heatproof bowl. Place the bowl over a saucepan of barely simmering water (without touching the water). Heat, stirring occasionally, until the chocolate and butter are melted and mixture is smooth. Do not allow the water to boil or the chocolate may scorch. Stir the rice krispies or cornflakes into the chocolate mixture. While still warm, spread the peanut butter crunch evenly over the dacquoise. Place in freezer until firm.

Prepare ganache: Melt the chocolate in a bowl over barely simmering water. Bring the cream to a boil; then gradually whisk into the chocolate.

Assemble the cake: Using a serrated knife, cut the chocolate cake in half horizontally to form 2 layers. Spread one third of the ganache on top of the bottom half. Remove the dacquoise from the freezer and peel off the parchment paper. Place dacquoise (peanut butter crunch side up) on top of ganache-covered cake. Gently press to remove any air pockets. Spread half of the remaining ganache over the peanut butter crunch. Place second half of cake on top. To allow for easy trimming, place cake in freezer until set, about 1 hour, and as much as one day in advance. Remove from freezer and using a serrated knife carefully trim off the rough edges of the cake to form a rectangle with neat, clean sides. Re-warm the remaining ganache over a pot of simmering water and spread over the top of the cake allowing some to drip a little over the sides.

Prepare whipped milk chocolate ganache: Melt chocolate in a bowl over barely simmering water. Bring the cream to a boil; then gradually whisk into the chocolate to combine. Must be refrigerated overnight. Whip the ganache slowly and gently (careful not over whip or it will become grainy.) Spoon the whipped milk chocolate ganache on each piece of cake. Top with almond and a strip of chocolate décor.

GRAMERCY
TAVERN

pastry chef
Nancy Olson

www.gramercytavern.com

sugar cookies

1 cup butter

1 cup sugar, plus extra for coating

1 vanilla bean, scraped

1 tablespoon corn syrup

2 eggs

3 ¾ cups flour

2 teaspoons baking soda

1 teaspoon baking powder

1 teaspoon salt

strawberry ice cream (yields 2 quarts)

1 ½ pounds whole strawberries, hulled

1 tablespoon lemon juice

2 cups sugar, divided

1 ¼ cups heavy cream

1 ¼ cups milk

10 egg yolks, whisked

2 teaspoons vanilla extract

Pinch of salt

blackberry ice cream (yields 2 quarts)

1 ½ pounds blackberry

½ cup sugar

2 cups sugar, divided

1 ¼ cups heavy cream

1 ¼ cups milk

10 egg yolks

2 teaspoons vanilla extract

Pinch of salt

2 tablespoons blackberry liqueur

summer ice cream sandwich poppers

YIELDS 25 ICE CREAM SANDWICHES — ADVANCE PREPARATION REQUIRED

Prepare sugar cookies: Preheat oven to 325°F and position a rack in the center. In a stand mixer fitted with a paddle attachment, cream together the butter, sugar, and vanilla bean. Add the corn syrup and eggs. Add the flour, baking soda, baking powder, and salt to the butter mixture and mix only to incorporate, scrape the sides of the bowl with a rubber spatula. Using a teaspoon, scoop the batter out into a bowl of granulated sugar and toss to coat the outside of the cookies. Place the balls onto a parchment paper lined sheet tray. Flatten with the palm of your hand to about half-inch in diameter rounds. Bake 5 to 8 minutes, or until edges turn golden. Set aside to cool.

Prepare strawberry ice cream: The night before, combine the whole strawberries, lemon juice, and ½ cup sugar in a bowl, cover, and store in the refrigerator. The next day, bring cream, milk, and 1½ cups sugar to a boil; remove from the heat. Place egg yolks in a large bowl, and slowly whisk in the hot cream mixture, being sure not to scramble. Return mixture to the pot, and cook on low heat, whisking, to reach 170°F. Pour mixture over the prepared strawberries. Puree with a hand blender until smooth. Strain the base through a fine meshed sieve, add the vanilla extract and salt, and chill well. Place into an ice cream machine and freeze according to the manufacture's directions. Place in freezer overnight to harden.

Prepare blackberry ice cream: The night before, combine the black berries and ½ cup sugar in a bowl, cover, and refrigerate. The next day, bring cream, milk, and 1½ cups sugar to a boil; remove from the heat. Place egg yolks in a large bowl, and slowly whisk in the hot cream mixture, being sure not to scramble. Return mixture to the pot, and cook on low heat, whisking, to reach 170°F. Pour mixture over the prepared blackberries. Puree with a hand blender until smooth. Strain the base through a fine meshed sieve, and add the vanilla, salt and blackberry liqueur; chill well. Place into an ice cream machine and freeze according to the manufacture's directions. Place in freezer overnight to harden.

Assembly: Once the cookies are cool, place in freezer to chill. Place a tablespoon scoop of the strawberry ice cream between two of the cookies and gently press together. Immediately place back into the freezer to prevent melting. Repeat with the blackberry ice cream and assemble all cookies.

pastry chef
Jennifer Giblin

www.bluesmoke.com

chocolate chip cookies with sea salt

1 cup butter

1½ cups + 2 tbls granulated sugar

1 egg + 1 egg yolk

1 teaspoon vanilla paste
(or vanilla extract)

⅔ teaspoon baking soda

1 teaspoon coarse sea salt

2 ⅔ cups all-purpose flour

10 ½ ounces dark chocolate, chopped

In a standing mixer fitted with a paddle attachment, cream the butter and sugar until smooth. In a small bowl, whisk together whole egg, egg yolk, and vanilla paste and add to the butter in three additions, scraping the sides and bottom of the bowl with a rubber spatula each time. Sift baking soda and flour together and add to the butter-egg mixture. Mix just until combined. Add the chopped chocolate. Scoop using a mechanical ice cream scoop the size of a golf ball onto a parchment paper lined baking sheet, leaving about 2 inches of space in-between. Refrigerate overnight.

Preheat the oven to 325ºF and place a rack in the center. Bake the cookies until lightly golden brown and still soft in the middle, about 8 to 10 minutes. Let cookies rest for a few minutes on the baking sheet before removing to a baking rack to cool.

52

small things SWEET

THE GENERAL GREENE

chef - owner

Nicholas Morgenstern

www.thegeneralgreene.com

vanilla cheesecake

3 pounds cream cheese

1 cup sour cream

2 vanilla beans, scraped

1½ cups sugar

6 eggs

1 cup heavy cream

poached rhubarb

6 rhubarb stalks

2 cups cranberry juice

¼ cup sugar

¼ cup grenadine

rhubarb jelly

4 sheets gelatin

2 cups rhubarb juice

½ teaspoon agar-agar

lime sugar

1 cup sugar

1 tablespoon lime juice

Zest of 2 limes

lemon-lime curd

1 gelatin sheet

1 egg yolk

4 eggs

1 cup sugar

½ cup lemon juice

¼ cup lime juice

Zest of 2 limes (reserve fruit for garnish)

6 tablespoons butter, cold

rhubarb cheesecake

YIELDS 24 TWO-INCH CHEESECAKES

Prepare vanilla cheesecake: Preheat oven to 250°F. In a stand mixer fitted with a paddle attachment, combine cream cheese, sour cream, vanilla beans, and sugar on low speed. Add eggs one by one, combine in-between each addition; then stream in the heavy cream to combine. Transfer to a 13 x 18 x 1" baking pan lined with a silpat. Place pan in the center of a larger baking or roasting pan and pour enough warm water into the larger pan to reach 2/3 of the way up the sides of the smaller pan. Bake for 50 minutes, or until set. Remove from the water bath; cool and freeze. Cut into two-inch rounds.

Prepare poached rhubarb: Peel the rhubarb (reserving the peel) and cut the stalks into two-inch pieces. Cut each piece through the middle on a lengthwise bias to make a triangle. Transfer triangles to a saucepot with the peel, cranberry juice, sugar, and grenadine. Boil for 5 minutes and strain through a fine meshed sieve. Discard peel. Return the liquid and rhubarb triangles to the pot. Cook the rhubarb for about 5 minutes at a slow simmer. Strain and chill the rhubarb; reserve rhubarb juice for jelly.

Prepare rhubarb jelly: Submerge the gelatin sheets in a bowl of cold water for 10 minutes; remove and squeeze out excess water. Line a lipped baking sheet with plastic wrap. In a pot, bring rhubarb juice and agar-agar to a boil, stirring. Cool slightly and stir in the gelatin to dissolve. Pour onto the cookie sheet and refrigerate for at least 2 hours; or until set. Cut out 2-inch rounds.

Prepare lime-sugar: Mix together the sugar, lime juice and zest and dry in a low oven. Break into small pieces.

Prepare lemon-lime curd: Submerge the gelatin sheet in a bowl of cold water for 10 minutes; remove and squeeze out excess water. Place the egg yolk, eggs, sugar, and lemon juice in a heat-proof bowl and place on top of a pot of simmering water (without touching the water). Cook; whisking until thick; remove from heat. Add zest. Stir in gelatin until dissolved. Strain through a fine meshed sieve into the bowl of an electric mixer and mix with the paddle attachment. On low speed, add butter in stages until cooled and well combined.

To serve: Place the jelly round on top of the cheesecake round. Decorate the jelly as well as the plate with poached rhubarb, lemon lime curd, fresh lime segments, and lime sugar.

dovetail
new york

pastry chef
Vera Tong

www.dovetailnyc.com

coconut caipirinha base

11 ounces baby coconut juice
(or canned unsweetened)

2 ounces cane syrup

2 ounces cachaça

1 teaspoon xanthan gum powder

mint basil foam

10 mint leaves

5 basil leaves

2 ounces Coconut Caipirinha Base
(recipe above)

8 kumquats

⅛ teaspoon xanthan gum

kumquat sugar

Finely grated zest of 10 kumquats

¼ cup sugar

garnish

Lemon juice, as needed

6 whole kumquats, cut into quarters,
seeds removed

8 mint sprigs

8 kumquat halves split ¾ through

coconut caipirinha with kumquats

YIELDS EIGHT SHOT GLASS SIZE SERVINGS

Prepare coconut caipirinha base: Combine the coconut juice, cane syrup, and cachaça in tall slender container. Blend with a hand immersion bender. Add xanthan gum, a few grains at a time while blending. Continue blending for 2 minutes or until mixture thickens. Keep chilled.

Prepare mint basil foam: Combine the mint leaves, basil leaves, Coconut Caipirinha Base, and kumquats in tall slender container. Blend with a hand-held immersion blender until smooth. Strain mixture though fine meshed strainer. Transfer to a clean tall slender container. Blend again with immersion blender adding xanthan gum a few grains at a time until mixture thickens. Keep chilled.

Prepare kumquat sugar: Combine zest and sugar and reserve for rimming shot glasses.

Assembly: Wet rims of 8 shot glasses with lemon juice and dip in kumquat sugar to delicately coat rims. Fill the shot glasses halfway with the Caipirinha base. Suspend three kumquat quarters in each glass. Foam mint and basil mixture with a hand-held immersion blender and spoon foam bubbles over Caipirinha base in glasses. Garnish rims with a split kumquat half and a mint sprig.

executive pastry chef
Kimberly Bugler

www.21club.com

polenta fritter

1 quart whole milk

1 cup sugar, divided

1 vanilla bean, split

1 cinnamon stick

1½ cups white polenta

½ cup mascarpone cheese

¼ cup heavy cream

1½ cups all-purpose flour

8 egg whites, lightly beaten

4 cups panko crumbs

rhubarb jam

3 cups small-diced rhubarb
(about 4 to 6 stalks)

½ cup sugar

1 teaspoon cornstarch

2 tablespoons lemon juice

garnish

1 cup Rhubarb Jam (recipe above)

1 fresh mango, cut into small julienne

Zest of 1 lime

1 piece of spun sugar (optional)

sweet polenta fritter
with rhubarb jam and mango

YIELDS **24** SERVINGS

Prepare polenta fritter: In a saucepot, combine milk, 3/4 cup sugar, vanilla and cinnamon. Heat to a simmer then slowly whisk in the polenta. Whisk until smooth, reduce heat as low as possible and cook gently for 8 minutes. Remove from heat and whisk in the remaining 1/4 cup sugar, mascarpone and heavy cream. Whisk until smooth. Spread mixture 1/2-inch thick onto a parchment lined baking tray. Refrigerate for one hour, until firm. Cut the polenta into (24) 1-inch squares. Dust the polenta squares lightly in flour then dip into egg whites and then into the panko crumbs. Fill a medium heavy-bottomed pot 1/3 way full with vegetable oil. Heat to 350°F; add the polenta squares in batches and deep fry until golden brown. Remove from the oil with a spider or slotted spoon, then strain and cool on paper towels.

Prepare rhubarb jam: Place the rhubarb and sugar in a medium saucepot. Dissolve the cornstarch in the lemon juice and add to the pot. Cook at medium heat until reduced and thick, about 5 to 10 minutes. Set aside to cool completely.

Assembly: Top each polenta square with a teaspoonful rhubarb jam, fresh cut mango, lime zest and spun sugar. Sauce the plate with some of the rhubarb jam thinned with water.

PARK AVENUE
SUMMER

executive pastry chef
Richard Leach

www.parkavenyc.com

1 cup (2 sticks) butter, cold, cubed

2 ½ cups flour

1 tablespoon sugar

Pinch of salt

6 tablespoons buttermilk

cherry filling

8 ounces (about 1¼ cup) sour cherries

¼ cup sugar

2¼ teaspoons cornstarch

½ teaspoon lemon juice

1 teaspoon Kirsch

Pinch of salt

Heavy cream

Sugar

BLUEBERRY CRUMB PIE

½ cup (1 stick) butter

1¼ cup flour

½ tablespoon sugar

Pinch of salt

3 tablespoons buttermilk

blueberry filling

8 ounces blueberries

2½ tablespoons light brown sugar

⅛ teaspoon grated nutmeg

½ teaspoon cornstarch

Pinch of salt

1½ teaspoons lemon juice

streusel topping

7 tablespoons butter

1 cup flour

3 tablespoons dark brown sugar

½ cup sugar

½ teaspoon each cinnamon and salt

trio of mini pies

YIELDS TEN OF EACH PIE

cherry lattice pie

Prepare pie dough: Combine flour, sugar and salt in bowl of stand mixer with paddle attachment. Add butter to flour mixture and mix until butter is very small pieces. Add buttermilk and mix just to moisten. Gather dough together and divide into 2 pieces. Wrap each piece with plastic wrap and chill for at least 1 hour. Remove 1 piece of dough from refrigerator and let stand at room temperature for 10 minutes. Roll dough on a floured surface to ¼ inch thick. Repeat with remaining dough. Using a 2-inch round cookie cutter, cut half the dough into 10 rounds, chill rounds for 5 to 10 minutes. Line 10 – 1¾ inch pie pans with the rounds of dough; being sure to press the dough into the bottom edges of the pans. Chill until ready to use. Using a pizza wheel, cut the other piece of dough into ¼ inch strips. Remove every other piece and gently place on a floured surface. Use the cut strips to assemble a basket weave. Cut the lattice with a 2¼ inch round cookie cutter. Chill until ready to use.

Prepare cherry filling: Wash and pit the cherries. Toss the remaining ingredients with cherries and set aside at room temperature for 15 minutes.

Assemble pies: Preheat oven to 400°F. Spoon cherry mixture into prepared pie shells. Top with lattice. Fold bottom crust over the edge of lattice and pinch closed. Brush tops with cream and sprinkle with sugar. Bake for 20 minutes; until juices are bubbling and crust is golden brown.

blueberry crumb pie

Prepare pie dough: Cut butter into small cubes and chill. Combine flour, sugar and salt in bowl of stand mixer with paddle attachment. Add butter to flour mixture and mix until butter is very small pieces. Add buttermilk and mix just to moisten. Gather dough together, wrap in plastic wrap and chill for at least 1 hour. Remove the dough from refrigerator and let stand at room temperature for 10 minutes. Roll dough to ¼ inch thick. Using a 2-inch round cookie cutter, cut out 10 rounds of dough, chill rounds for 5 to 10 minutes. Line 10 – 1¾ inch pie pans with the rounds of dough being sure to press the dough into the bottom edges of the pans. Chill until ready to use.

Prepare blueberry filling: Wash blueberries and remove stems. Add remaining ingredients to berries, stir and gently press to release some juices. Set aside at room temperature for 15 minutes.

Prepare streusel topping: Melt and cool butter. Stir together remaining ingredients. Add melted butter to dry ingredients and blend together with fingers to form crumbs. Spread crumbs out on sheet tray and chill.

Assemble pies: Preheat oven to 400°F. Spoon blueberry filling into prepared pie shells and top with approximately 1 tablespoon streusel topping. Bake approximately 20 minutes, until juices are bubbly.

RECIPE CONTINUES ON PAGE 151

craftsteak | *new york*

pastry chef

Erica Leahy

www.craftrestaurant.com

roasted fig tart

1 whole wheat pastry dough

1 cup sifted all-purpose flour

¾ cup sifted whole wheat flour

1½ teaspoons sugar

¾ teaspoon salt

¼ cup cold butter, small cubes

4-6 tablespoons ice cold water

Wild Flower honey, as needed

figs

2 pints medium Black Mission Figs

Olive oil, as needed

Brandy, as needed

spiced sugar mixture
(combined and set aside)

¾ cup sugar

½ teaspoon ground cardamom

½ teaspoon ground coriander

½ teaspoon ground cinnamon

Prepare pastry dough: Toss the dry ingredients in a bowl with the cubed butter and chill for one hour. Place ingredients in bowl of stand mixer fitted with the paddle attachment, and mix on speed 1 until a fine crumb forms. With machine running, add cold water, a spoonful at a time until a dough forms and pulls away from the walls of the bowl. Note: If you do not have a stand mixer you may use a food processor, pulsing the dry ingredients and butter, and then slowly incorporating the water to form the dough. Turn dough out onto a lightly floured surface, shape into a flat round, wrap with plastic and chill 2 hours or overnight.

Once chilled, roll the dough out to about $\frac{1}{16}$ inch thick, and cut rounds using a $2\frac{2}{3}$ inch cookie cutter. Place the rounds on a flat surface and shape. To shape, create a square of each round by folding the top, sides, and bottom edges inward. The corners will create small open spaces. Do not flatten or pinch. Working with one square at a time, place dough over the opening of the paper-lined muffin cup with the folded side facing upwards. Press gently downward in the center of the dough, fitting the dough into the cup. Preheat oven to 350ºF. Chill shells 30 minutes. Par bake until 90% done (about 15 minutes), cool slightly. Remove shells from pan and place on a baking sheet lined with parchment.

Prepare figs: Lightly brush the skin of each fig with olive oil, stem, and neatly quarter each fig. Arrange the wedges flesh edge up, brush or sprinkle with brandy. Preheat oven to 375ºF. First place a drop of honey in the center of each shell. Fit each shell with 3 to 4 wedges of fig (if the figs are large you may need to cut wedges thinner). Be careful not to crack your shell as you work. The stem ends should be pointing up and out, think of them as flowers or leaves and arrange them decoratively. Sprinkle the figs with the sugar mixture and place the baking sheet in preheated oven. The figs will begin to roast, once the flesh is glistening and the tip edges crisp a little, remove from the oven and cool to a warm temperature; serve.

executive pastry chef
Elishia Richards

www.esca-nyc.com

apple cannoli

YIELDS 18 SERVINGS — ADVANCE PREPARATION REQUIRED

12 Granny Smith apples,
cored and not peeled

2 cups sugar

Juice of 4 lemons

4 cups white wine

½ cup brandy

2 cups water

cannoli cream

1 pound ricotta cheese

1 cup sugar

1 teaspoon of vanilla

¼ cup semi-sweet chocolate chips

flake pastry cookies

2 ½ flake puff pastry sheets, 12 x 14"

Sugar, as needed

Place apples standing upright in one layer in a large saucepan (you may need to do this in batches depending on pan size). Coat with sugar making sure some sugar is in the core. Add the lemon juice, wine and brandy partially covering apples and bring to a full boil for 5 minutes. Flip the apples, lower heat and simmer for 10 minutes. When apples are soft to touch, but not mushy, transfer apples to a shallow baking pan; set aside. Continue to simmer the liquid to a light syrup. Strain syrup through a fine meshed sieve; cool to room temperature. Pour syrup over apples, cover and refrigerate.

Prepare cannoli cream: Drain the ricotta cheese in a sieve in the refrigerator overnight until very dry. In the bowl of an electric mixer fitted with a whisk attachment, mix the ricotta, sugar and vanilla at high speed for 10 minutes. Add the semi-sweet chocolate chips and mix until combined. Cover and refrigerate.

Prepare flake pastry cookies: Preheat oven to 350°F. Place puff pastry on a baking sheet lined with parchment paper. Slice the pastry sheet in half. Make twelve strips for each side of sheet. Lightly sprinkle top of pastry with sugar. Bake for 12 to 15 minutes or until golden brown.

Assembly: Remove apples, reserving syrup, and slice into 6 rounds. For each serving, place two pastry cookies on a flat dish and place on top an apple slice followed by a layer of cannoli cream; repeat to make three alternating layers, finish with a pastry cookie. Top off with a scoop of vanilla ice cream and drizzle with some syrup from the apples. Plates can be decorated with chocolate and raspberry syrup.

Rossini's

manager

Peter Serpica

www.rossinisrestaurant.com

sesame paste

230 grams white sesame seeds, toasted

50 grams sesame oil

sesame sponge

120 grams Sesame Paste
(recipe above)

125 grams egg whites

80 grams egg yolks

40 grams tupelo honey

40 grams sugar

20 grams flour

2 grams salt

pineapple

1 pineapple

165 grams white wine

350 grams sugar, divided

65 grams tupelo honey

1 vanilla bean, scraped

5 grams Szechuan peppercorns

2 grams salt

yogurt sorbet

410 grams sugar

90 grams atomized glucose

6 grams ice cream stabilizer

4 grams salt

670 grams water

500 grams Greek yogurt

garnish

Black sesame seeds

Shiso

sesame sponge with tupelo honey, pineapple and yogurt sorbet

YIELDS TWELVE SERVINGS — ADVANCE PREPARATION REQUIRED

All measurements are in metric for the purposes of accuracy, conversion tables can be found online, but we don't recommend converting the measurements.

Prepare sesame paste: Put the sesame seeds in a high-powered blender and puree with the sesame oil to make a fine paste.

Prepare sesame sponge: Puree all ingredients in a blender until smooth. Strain through a fine meshed sieve and place the mixture into an iSi Cream Whipper. Close and charge with two nitrous oxide cartridges. Poke several holes in the bottom of a plastic pint container and spray mixture half way up. Microwave uncovered for 40 seconds. Tear cake into organically shaped pieces.

Prepare pineapple: Peel and core the pineapple then cut into a large dice; set aside. In a saucepan, heat the white wine, with 100 grams of the sugar, honey, vanilla and Szechuan peppercorns, until the sugar is dissolved. In a dry pan, add the remaining 250 grams sugar and melt until golden brown (dry caramel) remove from the heat and carefully (it may spatter) pour in the wine syrup, stirring until smooth. Set aside to cool. Vacuum seal the pineapples with the cooled poaching syrup and cook sous vide at 75°C for 30 minutes.

Prepare yogurt sorbet: Combine all of the dry ingredients. Heat the water to 40°C and whisk in the dry ingredients. Heat the syrup to 85°C; then cool the syrup rapidly over a bowl of ice water to 20°C and let sit overnight. Mix the syrup into the yogurt with an immersion blender. Process in an ice cream freezer according to manufacturer's instructions.

To assemble: Place a piece of warm pineapple on each serving plate with the sesame sponge on top. Sauce the plate with the reserved poaching liquid. Next to the pineapple, place a quenelle of the sorbet on a bed of the black sesame seeds and garnish with shiso.

Blackbird

pastry chef
Tim Dahl

www.blackbirdrestaurant.com

goat cheesecake kataifi nests

YIELDS **24** SERVINGS

kataifi nests

1 package of kataifi dough, preferably Apollo, defrosted at room temperature, about 5 hrs.

½ pound unsalted butter, melted

¼ cup granulated sugar

Pinch of cinnamon

lemony goat cheese cake

9 ounces fresh goat cheese

⅓ cup sugar plus extra as needed

2 large eggs, separated

1 tablespoon all-purpose flour

1 tablespoon lemon zest

2 tablespoons vanilla extract

Jar of candied kumquats

Preheat oven to 325°F and position a rack in center. Carefully move dough onto a smooth, dry surface. Tear off one-quater of a bundle, and cover with plastic wrap and then a damp towel. Wrap the remaining dough in plastic and reserve in the freezer.

Arrange dough into 12-inch strips. Remove 1/8-inch thick bundle of strips, form into tightly coiled nests of 2-inch diameter rounds and place on parchment lined baking sheet. Brush well with some of the melted butter. Combine sugar and cinnamon and sprinkle each nest with a heavy dusting. Place another sheet of parchment paper on top of nests, then weigh them down with another baking sheet in order to keep the nest shape during baking. Bake for 10 to 15 minutes. Remove from oven and remove top baking sheet and paper, return nests to oven for an additional 5 to10 minutes or until golden brown. Cool to room temperature.

Prepare cheese cake: Preheat oven to 250°F and position a rack in the center. Grease a 9-inch cake tin, then sprinkle bottom and sides with sugar. In a medium mixing bowl, combine the goat cheese and 1/3 cup sugar and mix with a wooden spoon until no lumps remain. Add the egg yolks, flour, zest, and vanilla, mix until combined scraping down the sides of the bowl. In a stainless steel bowl of an electric mixer fitted with whip attachment, whip the egg whites and one tablespoon of sugar to stiff peaks. Gently fold into the goat cheese mixture. Pour cheesecake batter into prepared tin to three-quarter full. Place tin in a roasting pan and fill pan with hot water to come 1-inch up sides of cake tin. Bake in preheated oven until cheesecake is set, approximately 20 to 25 minutes. Cool to room temperature, then refrigerate for at least 4 hours.

When ready to serve, use a 1-inch round cutter, dipped into hot water each time, to cut out cheesecake rounds. Immediately place each one onto a prepared kataifi nest. Slice kumquats and place a half piece atop cheesecakes, drizzle with a few drops of candied syrup and serve immediately.

how *sweet* **it is**
N E W   Y O R K   C I T Y

chefs - owners
Beth Pilar   Ellen Sternau

www.howsweetitispastry.com

68

small things SWEET

shiso sorbet

1 cup sake

5 cups water

2 tablespoons atomized glucose

¾ cup sugar

100 red shiso leaves

Salt

Rice wine vinegar

pickled green mango

¾ cup rice wine vinegar

½ cup mirin

¼ cup sugar

¼ cup water

1 tablespoon grains of paradise

2 inch piece of fresh ginger, peeled and sliced

2 fresh Thai chilies

1 stalk lemon grass, bruised and sliced

Salt

2 unripe green mangoes

mango - grains of paradise tuile

1 ripe mango, peeled and core removed

Grains of paradise, as needed

grains of paradise jelly

2 sheets gelatin

1 teaspoon ground grains of paradise

½ cup sake

2 tablespoons sugar

garnish

Fresh mango, diced

Fresh red shiso, julienned

Micro shiso

shiso sorbet with mango & grains of paradise

YIELDS TWENTY SERVINGS — ADVANCE PREPARATION REQUIRED

Prepare sorbet: Bring the sake, water, glucose, and sugar to a boil. Add shiso leaves, remove from heat, cover and steep overnight in the refrigerator. Strain liquid through a fine meshed sieve and season with salt and rice wine vinegar to taste. Spin the sorbet in an ice cream freezer according to the manufacturer's instructions.

Prepare pickled green mango: Combine all of the ingredients except for green mangoes in a saucepot and bring to a boil. Peel and thinly slice the mangos using a mandoline. Place mango slices into the hot pickling liquid, remove from heat, cover and steep overnight in refrigerator. When ready to use, julienne mango as needed.

Prepare mango–grains of paradise tuile: Puree mango flesh in a blender until smooth; pass through a fine meshed sieve. Using an off-set spatula spread mango puree thinly onto a non-stick silpat lined baking sheet. Grind grains of paradise and sprinkle evenly over the sheet of puree. Place in a dehydrator overnight until completely dry. If a dehydrator is not available, tuiles can be dried in a 200°F oven for 24 hours. Remove sheet of mango and while still warm, slice into 2-inch strips with a large knife. Lift the strips one by one and using your fingers, twist into curls. If the strips become too brittle to twist, reheat until pliable. Dry at room temperature. Can be stored in an airtight container for 2 days.

Prepare grains of paradise jelly: Submerge the gelatin sheets in a bowl of cold water for 10 minutes; remove and squeeze out excess water. In a medium sized saucepot, heat 1/2 cup water and grains of paradise. Stir in the sake and sugar to dissolve, and then stir in the gelatin until dissolved. Transfer to a shallow baking dish or bowl. Chill in the refrigerator until set. Stir frequently while the gelatin is setting to disperse the spice in the jelly.

Assembly: Arrange fresh diced mango, julienned pickled mango and grains of paradise jelly on a plate. Place a scoop of shiso sorbet on the plate. Garnish with julienne of fresh red shiso, micro shiso, mango tuile and grains of paradise.

pastry chef
Della Gossett

www.charlietrotters.com

brittany shortbread

½ pound butter

1 teaspoon salt

1 pound plus 2 tablespoons flour

2 tablespoons baking powder

1 cup sugar

1 vanilla bean, split and scraped

white chocolate mousse

2 sheets gelatin

½ egg yolk

¾ cup of syrup 30 (3 oz sugar, 3 oz water simmered until dissolved and chilled)

7 ounces white chocolate, melted

1 pint whipped cream

White chocolate and cacao butter (optional)

Cocoa powder (optional)

lemon sorbet

3 cups sugar

⅓ cup atomized glucose

1 cup of water

1 quart of lemon juice

tuile

1 stick melted unsalted butter

½ pound sugar

½ cup flour

¾ cup orange juice

sugar decoration

½ cup isomalt sugar

1 teaspoon red color

white chocolate mousse, brittany shortcake, lemon sorbet, raspberry

YIELDS TEN SERVINGS — ADVANCE PREPARATION REQUIRED

Prepare brittany shortcake: In the bowl of an electric mixer fitted with a paddle attachment, cream the butter with salt until soft. Sift flour and baking powder together, and add to butter mixture to combine. In a separate bowl, whip egg yolks with sugar until pale and creamy; add vanilla beans. Add egg mixture to butter mixture on low speed until incorporated, being careful not to over mix. Wrap dough in plastic and chill overnight.

Preheat oven to 340°F. Flour a clean, flat surface, and using a rolling pin, roll dough into 1/10 inch thick sheets. Cut into (10) 3" x 1" rectangles and bake for 7 minutes; until golden brown.

Prepare mousse: Submerge the gelatin sheets in a bowl of cold water for 10 minutes; remove and squeeze out excess water. Combine egg yolk with syrup in a heat proof bowl and place over a bowl of simmering water (being sure the bottom doesn't tough the water). Whisk mixture until warm and thickened, then remove from heat and whip until cooled. Add melted white chocolate and gelatin stirring to dissolve. When the mixture reaches room temperature, fold in the whipped cream. Transfer mousse to a piping bag, and fill 4 plastic tubes (10-inch long/1-inch wide); freeze. Remove the frozen mousse from the plastic tubes, cut into (10) 3-inch long pieces. Spray frozen mousse with a mix of white chocolate/cacao butter (50/50). (Alternately, sift cocoa powder over the mousse-although this will result in a dark colored mousse). Refrigerate.

Prepare sorbet: In a small pot, bring the sugar, atomized glucose and water to a simmer. Cool, then add the lemon juice. Process in an ice cream machine according to manufacturer's instructions. Spread the sorbet into a cold frame or baking dish 1/2 inch deep; freeze. Cut into 3" x 1" rectangles.

Prepare tuile: Preheat oven to 375°F and position a rack in the center. In a medium bowl, whisk together the melted butter, sugar, flour, and orange juice. Spread the batter into a paper-thin layer onto a silpat-lined baking sheet and bake until lightly golden brown. Cut into 3" x 1" rectangles.

Prepare sugar decoration: Cook the sugar and red color in a saucepot to reach 340°F on a candy thermometer. Pour the sugar onto a silpat to stop the cooking. Using a spoon, scoop a bit of the sugar and let it stream in a very thin ribbon. Quickly stream the ribbon around a plastic tube or handle of a wooden spoon to make a coil shape. Allow the sugar to cool, and slide off of the tube. Repeat to use all of the sugar syrup. Cut coils into at least (ten) 3-inch long pieces.

RECIPE CONTINUES ON PAGE 150

adour
ALAIN DUCASSE

executive pastry chef
Sandro Micheli

www.adour-stregis.com

pandan butter cream

1 pound sugar

1 cup egg whites

2 pounds butter, room temperature, diced

2 teaspoons kosher salt

3 drops pandan extract (screwpine)

cake batter

4 ½ cups cake flour

2 tablespoons baking powder

1 ½ teaspoons kosher salt

1 ¾ cups unsalted butter, cold, diced

2 eggs

10 egg whites

1 ½ cups cream of coconut (preferably Aroy-d from Thailand in 560ml cans)

½ cup water

2 teaspoons coconut extract

2 teaspoons vanilla extract

Frozen pandan leaves, defrosted

to finish

¾ cup Sprite soda

Dried coconut

Rose petal jelly

pandan scented coconut layer cake

YIELDS NINE SERVINGS

Prepare pandan butter cream: Place sugar and egg whites in the bowl of a standing electric mixer and place the bowl on top of a pot of simmering water (being sure the bottom of the bowl does not touch the water). Heat, whisking, until the sugar is dissolved, then transfer the bowl to the mixer fitted with a whisk attachment. Whisk on medium speed, adding the diced butter in stages until cooled and well combined. Add the salt and pandan extract. Set aside at room temperature, covered, until ready to use.

Prepare cake batter: Preheat oven to 350°F and place a rack in the center. Sift flour, baking powder and salt together into the bowl of a standing electric mixer fitted with the paddle attachment. Add the cold butter and mix on slow speed until pea size crumbles form.

Place eggs, egg whites, cream of coconut, water and extracts in a bowl and whisk to combine. Take 2 cups of the liquid and stream into the flour mixture, beating until fluffy, then add remaining liquid until combined.

Grease (with butter) and flour a 10-inch round cake pan and line bottom with a round of parchment paper. Place a layer of pandan leaves in the bottom of the pan and pour batter over leaves. Bake for 45 minutes to an hour, until a toothpick comes out clean from the center of the cake. Cool at room temperature.

To finish: When cake is cool, remove from pan and slice horizontally into 3 even rounds, moisten each layer with about 1/4 cup of Sprite. Spread about 1/2 cup of butter cream on top of two layers then stack back together with the un-iced layer on top, Refrigerate to harden the buttercream, and then cut into 3-inch squares, ice the outsides, chill again, then pat with some dried coconut to coat.

Place a small pandan leaf on each plate with one piece of cake on top. Top with a dollop of rose petal jelly.

the Harrison

pastry chef

Colleen Grapes

www.theharrison.com

meringue

3 egg whites

½ cup granulated sugar

1 cup powdered sugar

strawberry syrup

15 ounces fresh strawberries, quartered

3 tablespoons sugar

1 vanilla bean, scraped

3 sprigs fresh mint

basil-lime sorbet

1 cup sugar

¾ cup each lemon and lime juice

1 cup (firmly packed) basil

lemon curd

¾ cup lemon juice

½ cup sugar

4 eggs

diplomat cream

2 cups milk

1 vanilla bean, scraped

7 egg yolks

½ cup sugar

4 tablespoons flour

4 tablespoons cornstarch

7 tablespoons butter, cold

1½ cups heavy cream

Zest from 1 lime

garnish

4 fresh strawberries, sliced thin

Fresh berries

"berries & cream"

Prepare meringue: Preheat oven to 200°F and place a rack in the center. Fill a small saucepot 1/3 with water, and bring to a light simmer. Place egg whites and sugar in a medium stainless steel bowl and place on top of the pot (the bottom of the bowl should not touch the water). Continuously whip egg whites and both sugars until the mixture reaches 140°F. Transfer the egg white mixture to the bowl of an electric mixer fitted with a whisk and whip until cool and stiff peaks form. Transfer to a pastry bag fitted with a 1/2 inch tip. Line a baking sheet with parchment paper or silpat and pipe 6 circles approximately 2-inches in diameter. Pipe small dots with the remaining meringue. Bake for 30 minutes, or until the meringue rings are dry on the bottom. Cool and reserve in dry, covered container at room temperature until ready to assemble.

Prepare strawberry syrup: Combine the strawberries, sugar, vanilla bean, and mint in a heat-proof bowl and place on top of a pot of simmering water (without touching the water) for 10 minutes to allow the sugar to extract juice from the berries. Strain the liquid into a small pot, discarding the strawberries, and simmer until reduced to a syrup; chill.

Prepare basil-lime sorbet: Bring sugar and 2 cups of water to a boil to dissolve the sugar; cool. Add the lemon and lime juice. Place the picked basil in a blender and puree with enough of the lemon and lime mixture to liquefy and combine, Strain though a fine meshed sieve into remaining liquid. Process in an ice cream freezer according to the manufacturer's instructions.

Prepare lemon curd: Combine lemon juice, sugar and eggs in a heat-proof bowl. Bring a small pot filled 1/3 with water to a simmer and place the bowl on top (without touching the water). Cook, whisking constantly, until thick enough to hold the marks of the whisk. Strain through a fine meshed sieve and set aside to cool.

RECIPE CONTINUES ON PAGE 151

BISTRO LAURENT TOURONDEL

pastry chef
TJ Obias

www.bltfish.com

marshmallow

10 sheets gelatin

2 ½ cups sugar

1 cup water

1 ¼ cups corn syrup

2 tablespoons raspberry flavoring

Powdered sugar, for dusting

chocolate sable

½ cup (1 stick) butter

½ cup sugar

1 cup all-purpose flour

½ cup cake flour

⅓ cup cocoa powder

½ teaspoon baking soda

¼ teaspoon salt

1 egg

1 teaspoon vanilla extract

garnish

Fresh raspberries, halved

Milk chocolate, chopped

Chocolate and raspberry sauce

raspberry s'mores

YIELDS 12 SERVINGS — ADVANCE PREPARATION REQUIRED

Prepare marshmallow: Submerge the gelatin sheets in a bowl of cold water for 10 minutes; remove and squeeze out excess water. Place the sugar, water, and corn syrup into a dry pot. Bring to a boil over medium heat. Brush any moisture from the inner sides of the pot that accumulated to avoid crystallization. Place the gelatin into the bowl with a stand mixer fitted with the whisk attachment, and whip on low speed; gradually adding the hot sugar mixture. Increase the speed to high and add the raspberry flavoring. Continue mixing for approximately 5 minutes then pour into a greased cake pan to set overnight in the refrigerator. When the marshmallow is set cut into desired shapes and dust in powdered sugar.

Prepare chocolate sable: In a standing mixer fitted with the paddle attachment, cream the butter and sugar until smooth Sift the flours, cocoa powder, baking soda, and salt together and add to the creamed mixture. Mix on slow speed; then add the egg and vanilla extract. Transfer mixture to a piece of parchment paper, mold into a square and chill for one hour.

Preheat oven to 350°F. Roll the dough out on a flat surface to 1/8 inch thick. Cut out your desired shape and bake on a parchment paper lined baking sheet for 8 to 10 minutes.

To serve: Place a piece of sable on each plate and top with cut marshmallows; the higher you stack it, the greater the effect. Use a piece of milk chocolate to help support the stack. With a hand held torch, toast the marshmallow until golden. Garnish the plates with chopped chocolate, fresh raspberries, chocolate and raspberry sauce.

The Sea Grill

executive pastry chef

Michael Gabriel

www.patinagroup.com

coconut lemongrass rice pudding

1 ¾ cups milk

1 ½ cups coconut milk

¼ vanilla bean, split and scraped

⅓ cup plus 1 tablespoon sugar

⅓ cup jasmine rice

Pinch salt

1 ½ inch piece lemongrass, cut with slit

basil simple syrup

1 cup water

1 cup sugar

Small bunch of fresh basil, rinsed

pineapple sauce

1 pineapple

¼ cup sugar

¼ cup water

garnish

1 cup small diced pineapple

In a medium size pot, combine the milks, vanilla, sugar, rice, and salt and bring to a boil. Reduce heat to a simmer and then add the lemongrass. Simmer until pudding is thick and the rice is soft. Remove lemongrass and refrigerate; covered.

Prepare basil simple syrup: In a small saucepot, bring water and sugar to a boil; cool. In another pot, bring a few cups of water to a boil and place a bowl of ice water on the side. Boil the basil until slightly wilted; chill in the ice water. Drain and transfer basil to a blender with the simple syrup; puree until well combined. Strain through a fine meshed sieve and store in the refrigerator.

Prepare pineapple sauce: Using a knife, peel the skin from the pineapple and cut into quarters. Cut away the core and then cut into chunks. Place the pineapple chunks in pot with sugar and water, cover, and cook on medium-low heat, stirring occasionally, until tender. Puree with a hand blender and strain the mixture through a fine meshed sieve. Return the liquid to a simmer over low heat until thickened. Set aside to cool. Taste and if necessary, adjust with more sugar or simple syrup.

To serve: Mix the cup of diced pineapple with pineapple sauce, reserving some sauce for garnish. For each serving, scoop a heaping tablespoon of rice pudding onto spoon. Drizzle basil simple syrup onto rice pudding. Spoon a small amount of pineapple mixture on top of rice pudding. Dab a small amount of pineapple sauce and basil simple syrup on the plate.

Telepan

pastry chef

Larissa Raphael

www.telepan-ny.com

chocolate cake

1 ¾ cups sugar

1 ½ cups all-purpose flour

¾ cup cocoa powder

1 ½ teaspoons baking soda

¼ teaspoon baking powder

1 cup butter, very soft

1 ½ eggs

1 ⅓ cups warm water

chocolate mousse

1 quart heavy cream

1 pound dark chocolate, chopped

5 ounces milk chocolate, chopped

10 egg yolks

1 ¼ cups plus 2 tablespoons sugar

chocolate glaze

1 cup water

¼ cup sugar

6 tablespoons butter

14 ounces dark chocolate

4 egg yolks

bridge sides

1 ½ - 2 pounds fine dark chocolate, chopped, divided

bite size bridge

YIELDS APPROXIMATELY 70 PIECES — ADVANCE PREPARATION REQUIRED

Prepare chocolate cake: Preheat oven to 350°F and position a rack in the center. Butter and flour (or line with non-stick cooking spray and parchment paper) a 13 x 18 x 1" baking pan. In the bowl of an electric mixer fitted with a paddle attachment, combine the sugar, flour, cocoa powder, baking soda and baking powder. Add softened butter until and mix until moistened. Add eggs one at time, beating well between each addition. Scrape down sides of bowl and gradually add the water until well combined. Transfer batter to prepared baking pan and bake for 15 minutes; the cake should spring back to the touch. Set aside to cool.

Prepare chocolate mousse: In a bowl, whip the heavy cream to soft peaks; keep chilled until ready to use. Place both chocolates in a heat-proof bowl over a pot of simmering water (being sure that the bottom of the bowl does not touch the water), and heat, stirring occasionally to form a smooth slightly, thickened liquid. In an electric mixer fitted with a whisk attachment, whip egg yolks until pale yellow and the mixture folds over on itself forming ribbons. In saucepot, combine sugar and enough water to resemble wet sand. Scrape down sides of pot and over high heat, cook sugar to 248°F. Stream sugar syrup into yolks mixture, while whipping. Stop mixer and fold in with a rubber spatula to the melted chocolate. Fold in the whipped cream in stages, scraping bottom and sides of bowl between each addition. Pour mousse on top of chocolate cake and refrigerate overnight.

Prepare glaze: In a saucepot, combine water, sugar, and butter and bring to a boil. Turn off heat, whisk in chocolate then the egg yolks. Unmold the mousse topped cake and place on a rack set over a baking sheet. Pour warm chocolate glaze on top of cake and refrigerator for at least ½ hour.

To assemble: Cut the cake into 1" x 1¼" bite size slices. Place half of the chocolate in a heat-proof bowl over a pot of simmering water (being sure that the bottom of the bowl does not touch the water), stir occasionally. Heat to 118°F (using candy or instant read thermometer). Remove from heat; add ⅓ of the un-melted chocolate. Continue stirring and gradually add the remaining chocolate until cooled to 80°F. Warm the chocolate to a working temperature of 88° to 90°F. Fill paper cornet with chocolate and pipe desire decoration onto a sheet of parchment paper; let set. Once set, press two bridges on two opposite sides of the cake slices.

The River Café

pastry chef

Karen McGrath

www.rivercafe.com

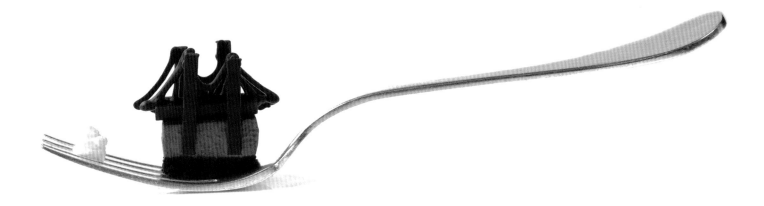

3 ½ cups plus 4 tablespoons cake flour

3 ¼ cups plus 2 tablespoons sucrose, divided

1 tablespoon salt

2 tablespoons baking powder

1 ¼ cups grapeseed oil

15 egg yolks

½ cup plus 2 tablespoons each: water, fresh orange juice and fresh yuzu juice

1 vanilla bean, scraped

Zest of 1 orange and 1 yuzu

16 egg whites

½ teaspoon cream of tartar

gelée tropicale

3 cups apricot puree*

¾ cup plus 2 tbls mandarin orange puree*

¼ cup passion fruit puree*

1 tablespoon fresh yuzu juice

¼ cup plus 2 tablespoons simple syrup

1 ½ sheets gelatin

cocoa mikado

1 cup plus 2 tablespoons simple syrup

2 tablespoons glucose syrup

2 cups cocoa powder

lychee black tea cremoso with bergamot

1 cup plus 1 tablespoon full fat milk

1 cup plus 1 tablespoon cream (35% fat)

¼ cup dry lychee black tea

5 egg yolks

1 pound 32% milk chocolate (preferably Amedei Toscano Brown brand)

4 ¼ teaspoons bergamot juice

tea time

YIELDS 25 SERVINGS — ADVANCE PREPARATION REQUIRED

Prepare yuzu-orange paradiso: Sift together cake flour, 2 cups plus 2 tablespoons sucrose, salt, and baking powder; set aside. In a stand mixer fitted with a whisk attachment, whip egg yolks and grapeseed oil to combine. Mix in the water, orange and yuzu juice to egg yolk mixture and mix until fully incorporated; then add vanilla bean seeds, orange zest and yuzu zest and mix until incorporated. Set mixture aside. In another bowl, whisk together the egg whites, cream of tartar and remaining 1 ¼ cups sucrose to a firm peak (meringue). Gently fold egg yolk mixture into meringue; then gently fold in the sifted ingredients. Split the mixture between 2 sheet pans, and bake at 350°F for 10 minutes. Cool and freeze.

Prepare gelée tropicale: Submerge the gelatin sheets in a bowl of cold water for 10 minutes; remove and squeeze out excess water. Prepare simple syrup with equal parts water and sugar, dissolved. Combine the purees, yuzu juice and simple syrup. Take ¼ cup of the total liquid amount and warm in microwave; stir in gelatin until dissolved. Add juice-gelatin mixture to remaining liquid. Strain through a fine meshed sieve. Pour into a container with large surface area to make a ¼" thick gelée.

Prepare cocoa Mikado: Prepare simple syrup with equal parts water and sugar, dissolved. Heat simple syrup and glucose syrup in medium pot to reach 140°F. Slowly whisk in cocoa powder to form a paste. Strain through a fine mesh strainer into a bowl or container set over another bowl of ice water, and stir occasionally until well chilled. Transfer mixture to piping bag.

Prepare lychee black tea cremoso: Combine cream and milk with tea and infuse overnight; strain. Bring infused milk and cream to a boil. Slowly whisk hot cream into egg yolks, being careful not to scramble. Strain yolk mixture through a fine meshed sieve over chocolate. Add bergamot juice. Puree with a hand immersion blender to create a smooth texture. Refrigerate to set.

*You may use frozen purees with 10% sweetness (ex. Perfect Puree or Boiron Brands)

RECIPE CONTINUES ON PAGE 152

pastry chef
Gabriele Riva

www.noburestaurants.com

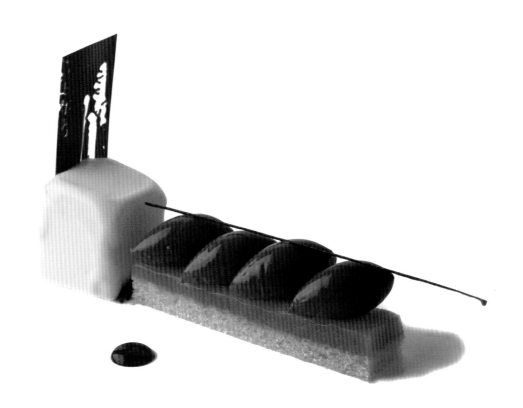

frrrozen hot chocolate ice cream

YIELDS ONE GENEROUS PINT — ADVANCE PREPARATION SUGGESTED

2 large egg yolks

⅓ cup sugar

1 package *Serendipity Frrrozen Hot Chocolate mix or ½ cup hot chocolate mix

2 cups half-and-half

½ teaspoon vanilla extract

*MIX CAN BE PURCHASED AT SERENDIPITY3.COM OR AT WILLIAMS-SONOMA STORES.

Combine the egg yolks and sugar in a heat-safe bowl of an electric mixer fitted with a whisk. Beat until thick and pale yellow, 3 to 5 minutes, and set aside. Combine the hot chocolate mix and half-and-half in a medium saucepan. Whisk until dissolved and then bring to a simmer over medium heat. Slowly stream half the hot chocolate mixture to the egg yolk mixture, while whisking on low speed. Whisk the yolk mixture into the pot of remaining chocolate mixture and return to low heat. Cook, stirring constantly for 5 to 10 minutes; until mixture is thick enough to coat the back of a spoon, or it reaches 170°F on a candy thermometer. Be extremely careful not to overheat, as it is easy to curdle egg yolks. Remove pan from heat and pour into a heat-safe bowl. Cover and refrigerate mixture until completely cold, preferably overnight. Add the vanilla extract and freeze in an ice cream maker according to manufacturer's instructions. Store in a plastic container in freezer.

RECIPE VARIATION: Extra Chocolate Frrrozen Hot Chocolate Ice Cream: Finely grate 2 ounces best-quality semisweet chocolate and mix into ice cream just before finished churning. (A microplane grater works well for shavings.)

Scoop into ice cream cones with your favorite topping.

small things SWEET

serendipity 3

owner - founder   executive chef

Stephen Bruce   Joe Calderone

www.serendipity3.com

almond, anise and orange biscotti
(biscotti di mandorle, anis e arancia)

YIELDS ABOUT FOUR DOZEN BISCOTTI

3 ½ cups unbleached all-purpose flour
(plus extra for shaping)

1 teaspoon baking powder

1 teaspoon kosher salt

4 cups whole, blanched almonds

4 large eggs

2 egg yolks, plus one egg white, reserved

2 cups granulated sugar

2 teaspoons pure vanilla extract

1 tablespoon whole anise seed

Freshly grated zest of 1 large orange

1 tablespoon granulated sugar, for glaze

Place the flour, baking powder and salt in a medium-sized mixing bowl and whisk to thoroughly combine ingredients. Using a sharp chef's knife, coarsely chop the whole almonds and set aside.

In the bowl of an electric mixer, fitted with the paddle attachment beat together eggs, egg yolks and 2 cups sugar on medium speed until light, about 2 minutes. The mixture will look somewhat curdled. Beat in the vanilla extract, anise seed and orange zest. Beat in dry ingredients, then the chopped nuts, to make a soft dough. Remove dough from bowl, wrap in plastic wrap and chill for 2 hours, or until firm enough to handle.

Preheat oven to 325°F. Lightly grease two cookie sheets with non-stick cooking spray or butter, or line with parchment paper. Divide the dough into five equal portions. On a lightly floured surface, shape each portion of dough into a log, about 1½" in diameter and 10" long. Place two logs on one baking sheet, 3" apart, and three logs on the second baking sheet. In a small bowl, beat egg white with a fork until frothy. With a pastry brush, glaze each log with beaten egg white and sprinkle with granulated sugar. Bake the logs until they are lightly golden brown, firm to the touch and just beginning to crack slightly, about 18 to 20 minutes. Rotate the pans 180° halfway through the baking time to ensure even browning.

Remove the baking sheets from the oven and reduce oven temperature to 200°F. Allow the logs to cool on baking sheet until cool to the touch, about 40 minutes. With a sharp, serrated knife, slice the biscotti, slightly on the bias, into ¼-inch wide slices. Lay the slices on baking sheets in single layer; return to oven and cook for 20 more minutes, or until the biscotti are toasted, dry and crisp. Cool completely on baking sheets, then store in an airtight container kept in a cool, dry place, for up to two weeks.

RISTORANTE

BABBO

ENOTECA

pastry chef
Gina DePalma

www.babbonyc.com

lemon curd

2 ¼ grams powdered gelatin

120 grams lemon juice

19 grams lemon zest

187 grams sugar

150 grams eggs

225 grams butter, softened

pistachio gioconde

375 grams eggs

281 grams powdered sugar

281 grams almond flour

75 grams all-purpose flour

50 grams pistachio paste

56 grams melted butter

247 grams egg whites

125 grams sugar

lemon robiola mousse

½ sheet gelatin

⅛ cup milk

Zest of one lemon

1½ tablespoons sugar

2 egg yolks

19 grams fresh robiola cheese

19 grams Lemon Curd (recipe above)

½ cup heavy cream, whipped to soft peak

lemon and robiola gateau, citrus marmalade, meyer lemon sorbet, cranberry caramel

YIELDS SIX SERVINGS — ADVANCE PREPARATION REQUIRED

All measurements are in metric for the purposes of accuracy, conversion tables can be found online, but we don't recommend converting the measurements.

Prepare lemon curd: Pour 10 grams of cold water into a small bowl and sprinkle gelatin evenly over top; rest for 5 minutes to saturate. In a medium saucepan, bring the lemon juice, zest and sugar to a simmer. Remove from heat, cover, and steep for 6 minutes. Strain through a fine meshed sieve into another saucepan. Crack the eggs into a heat proof mixing bowl, then slowly whisk the lemon juice into the eggs, being careful not to scramble. Return to the saucepan and over medium heat, whisk until thick, approximately 3 to 5 minutes. Immediately remove from heat and strain through a fine sieve into a mixing bowl. Add the softened butter and gelatin and whisk until smooth. Immediately cover with a sheet of plastic wrap adhering directly to the surface to avoid a skin, and chill for at least 2 hours.

Prepare pistachio gioconde: Preheat the oven to 400°F. In the bowl of an electric mixer fitted with a whisk attachment, whip together the eggs, powdered sugar, flours, pistachio paste, and melted butter; set aside. With the electric mixer, whisk the egg whites on medium speed until they start to froth. Then slowly pour the sugar into the egg whites, whisking to stiff peaks. Gently fold the egg whites into flour mixture, being careful not to deflate the whites. Spread batter approximately ¼ inch onto silpat-lined 13 x 18 x 1" baking pan and bake for 5 to 6 minutes, or until set to the touch. Set aside to cool completely. Cut into 4 x 1½" rectangular pieces and line the sides of six 2-inch ring molds. Cut a circle from remaining cake to fill the bottom of the ring molds.

Prepare lemon robiola mousse: Submerge the gelatin sheet in a bowl of cold water for 10 minutes; remove and squeeze out excess water. In a small saucepan, bring the milk and lemon zest to a simmer; add the sugar, stirring to dissolve. Put egg yolks in a mixing bowl and slowly whisk in the milk mixture, being sure not to scramble. Return mixture to the saucepan and cook over medium heat, stirring slowly with a wooden spoon until mixture thickens and will coat the back of the spoon. (You can test it by drawing a line with your finger on the back of the spoon and the custard will hold in place.) Remove from heat and strain through a fine sieve into a mixing bowl. Whisk in the robiola cheese, lemon curd, and gelatin. Place the mixing bowl over a larger bowl of ice water, and using a spatula, stir until cool. Fold in the whipped cream. Pour the custard into the gioconde-lined ring molds. Freeze overnight.

RECIPE CONTINUES ON PAGE 152

eighty one

pastry chef

John Miele

www.81nyc.com

crust

120 grams powered sugar plus extra for dusting

210 grams butter

3 grams salt

40 grams eggs

140 grams blanched almond flour

260 grams all-purpose flour

¼ teaspoon grapefruit zest

¼ teaspoon lime zest

½ teaspoon orange zest

filling

340 grams cream cheese, room temperature

115 grams sugar

1½ eggs

10 grams all-purpose flour

1½ teaspoons lemon juice

1½ teaspoons vanilla extract

100 grams strawberry puree

2 drops pink food color

garnish

Raspberry coulis

Freeze dried strawberry

strawberry cheesecake

All measurements are in metric for the purposes of accuracy, conversion tables can be found online, but we don't recommend converting the measurements.

Prepare crust: Preheat oven to 355°F. In the bowl of a standing mixer fitted with a paddle attachment, cream the sugar, butter, and salt. Add the eggs, mixing slowly to incorporate well. Add dry ingredients and combine well. Refrigerate. Roll up the dough 1/4-inch thick. Cut into rectangles the shape of the mold you will use for the cheesecake filling, sprinkle with powdered sugar and bake for 11 minutes, until golden brown.

Prepare filling: Preheat oven to 275°F. In a bowl, combine the cream cheese with the sugar. Whisk in the eggs then all the remaining ingredients. Transfer mixture to small rectangular flexipan molds*. Place mold in the center of a larger baking or roasting pan and pour enough warm water into the larger pan to reach 2/3 of the way up the sides of the smaller pan. Bake until firm, 35 to 45 minutes. Cool at room temperature and then chill in the refrigerator.

Serve cheesecake with raspberry coulis and freeze dried strawberry. A wild strawberry sorbet is recommended on the side.

* FLEXIPAN MOLDS AVAILABLE AT JBPRINCE.COM

Tribeca Grill

executive pastry chef

Stéphane Motir

www.myriadrestaurantgroup.com

coconut chocolate jasmine bombe

coconut mousse

2 sheets gelatin

1½ cups heavy cream

1 cup plus 2 tablespoons coconut puree

¼ cup sugar

jasmine tea disks

5.2 ounces chopped white chocolate

1½ teaspoons powdered jasmine tea

1½ cups Paillete Feuilletine
(crushed wafers)

chocolate jasmine ganache

½ cup cream

1 jasmine tea bag

1 tablespoon glucose

1.8 ounces chopped milk chocolate

4.8 ounces chopped 70% chocolate

Prepare coconut mousse: Place a one-inch silicone dome mold onto a large baking sheet. Submerge the gelatin sheets in a bowl of cold water for 10 minutes; remove and squeeze out excess water. Whip the cream until soft peaks form. Combine the coconut puree and the sugar in a heatproof bowl. Bring a small pot filled 1/3 with water to a simmer and place the bowl on top (without touching the water). Heat, stirring, until sugar is melted. Stir in the gelatin until dissolved. Cool coconut mixture slightly over a bowl of ice water until room temperature. Don't let it get too cold or you will have chunks of jelly in your mousse.

Fold the whipped cream into the coconut mixture until well combined. Transfer mousse to a pastry bag. Pipe the mousse into the domes slightly above the rim of the mold. With an offset spatula smooth the mousse so that the dome bottoms will be flat, removing any excess mousse. Freeze the domes for one hour. Using a small melon baller, scoop the inside of the domes creating small bowls. Return to freezer.

Prepare jasmine tea disks: Line a 13 x 18 x 1" baking pan with parchment paper and set aside. Put the chopped chocolate in a heatproof bowl. Bring a small pot filled 1/3 with water to a simmer and place the bowl on top (without touching the water). Stir the chocolate with a wooden spoon until just melted. Mix in powdered jasmine tea and then fold in the Paillete Feuilletine. Stir until well combined. Pour mixture onto the prepared pan and with an offset spatula press the mixture into the pan making sure it is evenly spread. Refrigerate for a few hours. Using a one-inch round cookie cutter, cut out as many rounds as possible. You can re-melt and spread the mixture one to two more times to cut more cookies.

Prepare chocolate jasmine ganache: Heat the cream, tea and glucose in a saucepan until hot, but not boiling. Steep the jasmine in the cream for five minutes. Squeeze the tea bag and remove from mixture. Pour the cream over the chocolates and stir until smooth. Transfer to a pastry bag.

Assembly: Pipe ganache into the middle of the coconut mousse bowls. Place one jasmine tea disk over each piped ganache. Put the domes back in the freezer for at least three hours. Unmold the bombes and place on a baking sheet. Once defrosted, you can garnish the bombe you can place one segment of a blackberry on top of each bombe or you can serve it as it is.

COCOA
BAKERY & BISTRO

chef – owner

Jessica Isaacs

www.cocoabakerycafe.com

pistachio madeleines

YIELDS 36 MADELEINES

½ cup (1 stick) unsalted butter
plus extra to grease pans

4 eggs

¼ teaspoon salt

⅔ cup sugar

1 teaspoon vanilla extract

1 cup all-purpose flour, sifted

4 tablespoons pure pistachio paste

Pistachio nuts, whole and chopped

Preheat oven to 375°F. Grease madeleine pans with butter then flour.

In a small saucepan, melt the butter over low heat; set aside to cool to room temperature. Whisk the eggs, salt, and sugar together until thick and airy, about 3 minutes. Add the vanilla extract. Quickly but gently, fold in the sifted flour, then thepistachio paste using a rubber spatula, mixing until combined. Gently fold in the melted butter, combine to thicken.

Quickly spoon mixture in the prepared madeleine pans. To add some crunch, sprinkle with some chopped pistachio nuts. Bake until golden, 12 to 15 minutes. Immediately unmold the madeleines while the pan is still warm.

Serve warm or room temperature on a plate garnished with whole pistachio nuts.

small things SWEET

chefs - owners
Florian Bellanger   Ludovic Augendre

www.madmacnyc.com

basil oil

1 bunch basil

1 pinch fine sea salt

1¾ cups vegetable oil, divided

tropical fruit dice

1 cup finely diced mango

1 cup finely diced pineapple

1 cup finely diced papaya

3 Thai basil leaves

1 gram (tiny pinch) fine sea salt

brick dough discs

3 sheets brick dough

Melted butter, as needed

Powdered sugar, as needed

lemon curd

½ cup lemon juice

3 eggs

3 egg yolks

½ cup sugar

Zest of 1 lemon

½ cup (1 stick) butter, cubed

pineapple sorbet with tropical fruit, lemon curd and thai basil

YIELDS EIGHT TO TEN SERVINGS — ADVANCE PREPARATION REQUIRED

Prepare basil oil: Bring a medium pot of water to a boil with sea salt and place a bowl of ice water on the side. Boil the basil for one minute; then remove with a slotted spoon to chill in the ice water. Remove basil from ice water and squeeze dry; chop roughly. Add ¼ cup of oil to a blender, top with basil, then remaining oil; cover. Puree on high speed for approximately three minutes to fully incorporate. From time to time, it is important to remove the lid from the blender to allow the steam to escape. Rapidly chill the oil by transferring to a bowl or container set over another bowl of ice water and stirring. Refrigerate oil until ready to use.

Prepare tropical fruit dice: Combine fruit in a medium sized mixing bowl. Finely, chiffonade three Thai basil leaves and add to the fruit. Season with sea salt. Cover and refrigerate until ready to use.

Prepare brickdough discs: Preheat oven to 325°F. Place one sheet of brick dough on to a cutting board. Brush with melted butter on both sides. Cut rounds about the size of a half-dollar, roughly 1¼ inches in diameter with a ring cutter. Sprinkle with powdered sugar and place the discs on to a sheet pan lined with a non-stick mat. Repeat with remaining sheets. Place another non-stick mat over the cut disc so they will remain flat during the baking process. Bake for 15 to 20 minutes or until golden brown.

Prepare lemon curd: Whisk the lemon juice, eggs, yolks, and sugar together. Strain through a fine meshed sieve into a heat-proof bowl. Add the lemon zest. Bring a pot filled ⅓ with water to a simmer and place the bowl on top (without touching the water). Whisk until mixture becomes pale, thick and resembles ribbons. Remove from the heat and gradually add butter, completely blending in-between each addition, until all of the butter is incorporated. Transfer curd to a baking pan and lightly cover with a sheet of plastic wrap to avoid a skin. Refrigerate to cool.

Evenly spread a small amount of curd on to a sheet pan, about a quarter inch thick. Place in the freezer until frozen, then cut 8 to 10 rounds to desired size with a 1¼-inch diameter ring cutter.

RECIPE CONTINUES ON PAGE 153

executive pastry chef

James Distefano

www.rougetomatenyc.com

pudding #1

- 4 cans (14 oz cans) condensed milk
- 2 teaspoons cream of tartar
- 5 eggs
- 16 egg yolks
- Scant ½ cup sugar
- 2 tablespoons Meyer lemon zest
- 2 ½ cups Meyer lemon juice
- ½ teaspoon salt

pudding #2

- 1 ½ cup plus 2 ½ tablespoons sugar
- 2 tablespoons cornstarch
- 6 eggs
- 2 egg yolks
- 10 fluid ounces Meyer lemon juice
- 2 tablespoons Meyer lemon zest
- ¼ teaspoon salt

lemon shortcrust

- 2 ½ sticks butter
- 1 cup packed light brown sugar
- 3 ½ cups all-purpose flour
- 1 ½ tablespoons Meyer lemon zest
- Pinch of salt

kaffir lime sorbet

- 2 ¼ cups milk
- 1 ½ cups sugar
- 7 large kaffir lime leaves
- 2 ¼ cups fresh squeezed lime juice

meyer lemon glass

- 2 ¼ cups Meyer lemon juice
- 1 ¼ cups sugar
- 1 tablespoon plus 1 teaspoon NH pectin

candied coriander seeds

- 2 ¼ cups sugar
- ½ cup dried coriander seeds

meyer lemon pudding

YIELDS 70 SERVINGS — ADVANCE PREPARATION REQUIRED

Prepare pudding #1: Preheat the oven to 275°F. Puree all ingredients in a blender or in a tall container using an immersion blender. Spray a very flat lipped baking sheet with non-stick spray, then line the bottom and sides with parchment paper. Pour the mixture on the pan and bake for 12 minute, then rotate 180 degrees and bake for another 10 minutes. The center should be set but still have a solid jiggle. Let custard cool at room temperature, then cover and refrigerate. While cooling, prepare the second pudding.

Prepare pudding #2: Fill a small saucepan halfway with water, and bring to a light simmer. Place all of the ingredients in a medium stainless steel bowl and place on top of the pot (the bottom of the bowl should not touch the water). Cook, whisking constantly until the mixture thickens, about 10 minutes. Strain mixture through a fine meshed sieve and pour into a lipped shallow pan to cool. Loosely place plastic wrap directly on top to avoid a skin. Chill in the refrigerator.

Prepare shortcrust: Preheat oven to 300°F and position a rack in the center. In the bowl of an electric mixer fitted with a paddle attachment, mix all ingredients together until it forms a smooth ball. Remove dough from mixer; wrap it in plastic wrap, refrigerate for 1 hour. Roll dough on a surface lightly dusted with flour until ¼ inch thick. Transfer dough to a parchment paper lined baking sheet and bake for 10 minutes, or until golden brown; cool. Then, using a sharp knife, chop the dough into tiny pieces. Set aside until ready to assemble.

Prepare kaffir lime sorbet: In a saucepan, bring 2 ¼ cups water, milk, sugar, and kaffir leaves to a simmer. Pour in a bowl over the lime juice, and set over another bowl of ice water, and stir occasionally until well chilled. Refrigerate overnight. The next day, strain, and spin in ice cream machine according to manufacturer's instructions.

Prepare Meyer lemon glass: Preheat oven to 180°F. In a saucepan, combine lemon juice, sugar, 1 ¼ cups water, and NH pectin. Bring to a boil over medium-high heat. Reduce heat and simmer for 3 minutes. Transfer the liquid to a bowl set over another bowl of ice water, and stir occasionally until well chilled. Once cool, strain through a chinois or fine meshed sieve. Using acetate, line a full sheet pan and spread a paper thin layer across entire pan. Transfer to oven. Keep in warm oven overnight to dry. The following day, peel the acetate from glass and break into shards for the décor.

RECIPE CONTINUES ON PAGE 153

GOTHAM
BAR AND GRILL

pastry chef
Deborah Racicot

www.gothambarandgrill.com

chocolate sable dough

2 egg yolks

1 stick (½ cup) butter

⅔ cup powdered sugar

⅛ teaspoon salt

⅛ cup almond flour

1¾ cups pastry flour

⅛ cup cocoa powder

milk chocolate black cherry and red peppercorn mousse

5 sheets gelatin

7 ounces chopped milk chocolate 40%

1¾ ounces chopped dark chocolate 72%

¾ cup glucose syrup

7 tablespoons black cherry puree

¼ teaspoon red peppercorn

¼ teaspoon fleur de sel

1½ tablespoons butter

1 cup whipped cream

Red cocoa butter spray*

chocolate decoration

1 pound dark Chocolate, chopped

garnish

Gold leaf

*RED COCOA BUTTER STRAY IS AVAILABLE AT LEPICERIE.COM

le temps des cerises

chocolate sable dough, milk chocolate, cherry and red peppercorn mousse

YIELDS ABOUT **50** SERVINGS

Prepare chocolate sable dough: Preheat oven to 325°F and position a rack in the center. Pour yolks into a cryovac bag, seal, and immerse in boiling water until cooked through, about 3 minutes. Chill bag in a bowl of ice water, remove yolks and pass through a strainer; set aside. In the bowl of an electric mister fitted with the paddle attachment, mix butter, powdered sugar, and salt to combine. Add the cooked yolks, almond flour, pastry flour, and cocoa powder. Remove dough, wrap in plastic wrap and refrigerate until firm and rested. Roll the dough on a surface lightly dusted with flour to ⅛ inch thick. Cut into desired size (use a 1" round cutter to cut out base) and transfer to a parchment paper-lined baking sheet. Bake for 10 minutes. Cool at room temperature.

Prepare milk chocolate black cherry and red peppercorn mousse: Submerge the gelatin sheets in a bowl of cold water for 10 minutes; remove and squeeze out excess water. Place chocolates and bloomed gelatin in a heat-proof bowl. Combine in a medium pot the glucose, black cherry puree, red peppercorn, and fleur de sel; bring to a boil, then pour over the chocolate. Stir to melt and combine. Blend with hand immersion blender until smooth. When the mixture cools to 95°F; add the butter. Fold in whipped cream. Fill 3½-inch long by 1-inch wide round tube with the mousse and freeze. Unmold and coat with crushed chocolate sable dough. Spray with red cocoa butter.

Temper chocolate: Place the chocolate in a heat-proof bowl over a pot of simmering water (being sure that the bottom of the bowl does not touch the water.) Melt the chocolate, stirring occasionally and continue to heat until it reaches 110°F to 115°F. Remove bowl from heat. Stir constantly with a spatula until the chocolate has reached 95°F to 100°F. Spread a paper thin layer of chocolate onto an acetate sheet. Cut and form into triangles and roll around a thin dowel to make "chocolate sleeves, before the chocolate sets.

Assembly: Stand chocolate garnish on top of the sable cookie and place mousse in the middle. Garnish with gold leaf.

Caravaggio

executive pastry chef

Philippe Muze

chocolate operetta

flourless chocolate cake

2 cups egg whites

1½ cups granulated sugar

1 cup egg yolks, beaten

¾ cup cocoa powder

coffee toffee buttercream

2 cups dark brown sugar

¾ cup light corn syrup

¾ cup water

1 tablespoon coffee extract or
2 tablespoons strong cold espresso

2 cups whole eggs

3 tablespoons melted bittersweet chocolate
(pourable consistency)

2 sticks of butter cubed, room temperature

chocolate glaze

10 ounces bittersweet chocolate, chopped

1 tablespoon vegetable shortening

¼ cup walnut or hazelnut oil

Prepare flourless chocolate cake: Preheat oven to 350°F and place a rack in the center. In a stand mixer fitted with a whip attachment, whisk the egg whites until lightly foamy. Gradually whisk in the sugar until starts to grow in size and becomes glossy (medium peak). Transfer the meringue into a large bowl. With a rubber spatula gradually fold in the egg yolks in three additions until all yolks are incorporated and meringue is uniform in color. Evenly sift the cocoa powder over top the meringue; fold to incorporate. Transfer batter to a silpat or parchment paper lined 13 x 18 x 1-inch baking pan and spread into an even layer. Bake for 10 minutes, rotate tray 180° and bake for an additional 5 minutes, or until a toothpick comes out clean from the center. Set aside to completely cool, then wrap and store in the freezer.

Prepare buttercream: In a tall heavy saucepan, bring sugar, corn syrup and water to reach 250°F on a candy thermometer (dark bubbles will start popping in 2 second intervals). Add the coffee extract and bring to 260°F, about 5 minutes. Remove from heat and cool to 240°F, about 10 minutes. Meanwhile, using a stand mixer fitted with a whisk attachment, whisk eggs until frothy. When sugar reaches 240°F, stream (towards the edge of the bowl) into the egg mixture while whisking on medium-high. Whip on medium speed for 1 minute, then stream in melted chocolate. Keep whisking until lukewarm; gradually add the butter until mixture cools down, light in color and slightly shiny. (If at any time it looks curdled, keep whisking, it will return to shiny and smooth looking.) Keep covered in a plastic container.

Prepare glaze: Fill a small saucepot 1/3 with water, and bring to a light simmer. Place the chocolate and shortening in a medium size heatproof bowl and place on top of the pot (the bottom of the bowl should not touch the water). Stir to melt chocolate and incorporate shortening. Keep warm.

To assemble: Spread all of the buttercream evenly on top of cake making sure all corners appear level. Transfer to freezer for at least one hour. Remove from freezer and pour the warm chocolate glaze on top of the center of cake all at once. The glaze must be spread quickly and evenly either with a flat metal spatula or by tipping and rotating pan to move the glaze to cover. Set aside for 30 minutes; then cut with a hot/warm knife into (50) 4 x 1-inch pieces. Store in the refrigerator, covered until ready to serve.

davidburke townhouse
AMERICAN CUISINE

pastry chef
Gustavo Tzoc

www.davidburketownhouse.com

concord grape cheesecake

2 cups fresh or organic Concord grape juice, reduced to 1 cup

1 pound + 4 ounces cream cheese

¼ cup + 1 tablespoon + 1 teaspoon sugar

2 tablespoons heavy cream

3 eggs

1½ teaspoons melted butter

2 tablespoons + 2 teaspoons sour cream

graham cracker crust

2 cups graham cracker crumbs

¼ cup sugar

½ cup butter, melted

pistachio tuile

½ cup butter

½ cup + 2 teaspoons sugar

3 egg whites

¼ cup + 1 tablespoon flour

¼ cup + 1 tablespoon pistachio flour

Crushed pistachios

garnish

Concord grapes

If using fresh grapes, remove them from the vine and grind in a food processor. Strain through a fine mesh strainer; measure and reduce. In a stand mixer fitted with paddle attachment, add the cream cheese and mix until soft. Add the sugar and mix. Stream in the heavy cream. Stop the machine and scrape down the sides of the bowl. Add the eggs one at a time, combining well after each addition. Add the melted butter, sour cream and grape juice; mixing until well incorporated. Scrape down the sides, strain batter through a fine meshed sieve and set aside.

Prepare crust: Preheat oven to 300°F. In a bowl, mix together the graham cracker crumbs and sugar. Add the melted butter and combine. Line a 7 x 9 inch pan with parchment paper then spray bottom and sides with nonstick cooking spray. Transfer the crumb mixture to prepared pan. Using the bottom of a cup, tap on the crumbs to get an even layer. Place in oven and bake for 10 minutes. Remove and pour the batter over crust. Place in the center of a larger baking or roasting pan and pour enough warm water into the larger pan to reach 2/3 of the way up the sides of the smaller pan. Place in oven and bake for 15 minutes then rotate the cheesecake and bake for another 15 minutes. Check for doneness by lightly tapping the side of the pan, the cheesecake should be set and not jiggle. If needed, bake an additional 10 to 15 minutes. Carefully remove from the oven. When cool to the touch, remove from the water bath and chill in the refrigerator. When cooled completely, using an oval cutter, cut into 12 portions.

Prepare pistachio tuile: Preheat oven to 300°F. In a small pot, melt the butter then add the sugar, stirring to dissolve. Remove from heat. Whip the egg whites in a stand mixer fitted with whisk attachment, until frothy. Add the butter-sugar mixture to mixer while whipping on low speed. Add the flours and whisk until no lumps remain. Chill in refrigerator. Spread onto a silpat in a very thin layer and cover with crushed pistachios. Bake for 7 minutes, or until light brown. Remove from the oven. While still hot, using an oval cutter, cut into 12 ovals. If the tuiles turn cold before finished cutting, return to oven for 5 minutes. Cool, and store in an airtight container until time of use.

To serve: Place one cheesecake in the center of each plate. Place a pistachio tuile off center. Cut two concord grapes in half and arrange on top of the cheesecake and on the side. Repeat for each serving.

pastry chef

Jacqueline Zion

www.theodeonrestaurant.com

geranium granité, rose scented cream, sicilian pistachio cup

YIELDS EIGHT SERVINGS

granité

2 cups water

¼ cup sugar

1 cup organic geranium petals

rose scented cream

½ cup heavy cream

1 tablespoon sugar

¼ cup organic rose petals

½ cup mascarpone

sicilian pistachio cup

½ cup Sicilian pistachios, finely minced

6 tablespoons sugar

1 tablespoon corn syrup

garnish

Fleur de sel

Sicilian pistachio paste

Sicilian pistachios

Prepare granite: Combine the water and sugar in a small saucepot and heat to approximately 190°F. Mix in the geranium petals, remove from heat and steep for 2 minutes. Strain and discard petals and pour the liquid into a plastic container; freeze uncovered. Every 25 minutes, carefully shave the ice crystals with a fork in a horizontal direction. Repeat this process until the crystals are completely solidified and fluffy.

Prepare rose scented cream: Combine heavy cream, sugar, and rose petals in a saucepan, gently warm until the rose perfumes the cream to the desired intensity (you can muddle the petals to help develop the scent). Strain out the petals, cool the cream, and whip to a very soft peak. Slowly whisk the cream into the mascarpone. Transfer to a small container, cover and chill in the refrigerator.

Prepare pistachio cup: Preheat oven to 300°F. Combine pistachios, sugar and corn syrup until well combined. Using your palms, roll mixture into eight equal balls. Place balls onto a sheet of silpat; leaving 3 inches of space in-between. Place a piece of parchment paper atop the pistachio ball and roll them as close to paper thin as possible, do not remove parchment paper. Transfer silpat to a baking sheet and freeze. Remove parchment paper and bake for approximately 12 minutes, until the sugar is melted. Cool slightly, and using an offset metal spatula carefully peel off the tuile and mold into a bowl by pressing into a cup; cool and reserve.

For each serving: Place the pistachio cup on a frozen plate or a frozen hand, spoon geranium granite onto the center, add one quenelle of rose scented cream, a small pinch of fleur de sel, and finish with a drizzle of Sicilian pistachio paste and a few whole pistachio nuts.

pastry chef
David Carmichael

www.giltnewyork.com

sake gelatin

3 sheets gelatin

1 cup simple syrup

1 cup sake

mango dice

1 fresh mango, small dice (equally sized)

dulce de leche ice cream

1 can (8 ounce) condensed milk

2 sheets gelatin

1 quart milk

1 cup egg yolks (about 11 yolks)

½ cup glucose syrup

7 ounces ice cream stabilizer

arroz con leche foam

½ quart milk

½ quart heavy cream

1 cinnamon stick

⅓ cup sugar

Peels of 1 orange and lemon

1 cup sushi rice

puff rice

4 cups water

1 cup white rice

Oil, for frying

Cinnamon

Powdered sugar

arroz con leche

YIELDS FOUR SERVINGS — ADVANCE PREPARATION REQUIRED

Prepare sake gelatin: Submerge the gelatin sheets in a bowl of cold water for 10 minutes; remove and squeeze out excess water. In a medium sauce-pot over low heat, gently warm the simple syrup to just below a simmer. Stir in the gelatin until dissolved. Add the simple syrup to the sake and stir well. Reserve, chilled.

Prepare dulce de leche ice cream: Submerge the condensed milk in a pot of water held just below a simmer for 8 hours. Cool before opening can. Submerge the gelatin sheets in a bowl of cold water for 10 minutes; remove and squeeze out excess water. Add the milk, glucose syrup, and egg yolks to a pot. Slowly heat, whisking until the mixture reaches 80°F. Add the stabilizer and gelatin, stirring to dissolve. Bring temperature up to 180°F and remove from heat. Add the condensed milk and blend with an immersion blender; chill. Process in an ice cream freezer according to instructions.

Prepare arroz con leche foam: Add the milk, heavy cream, cinnamon stick, sugar, and citrus peels to a saucepan to scald. Add the rice and cook slowly until tender. Remove and discard the peels and cinnamon sticks. Transfer to a blender, or food processor and puree until smooth. Strain through a fine mesh sieve. Chill, and transfer to a CO_2 sifon.

Prepare puff rice: Bring the water to a boil and add the white rice. Over-cook the rice and spread in flat layers onto parchment paper lined trays. Place in a warm dry area to dry out. Heat oil in a large pot to 350°F. Add a hand full of rice to the oil and as soon as it puffs and rises to the top, remove with a slotted spoon or fine meshed strainer, and drain rice on a paper-towel lined tray. Repeat this procedure with the remaining rice. Dust the puffed rice with cinnamon and powdered sugar. Reserve in a dry place.

To serve: Divide sake gelatin to the bottom of four chilled glasses. Top with a layer of diced mango. Add ice cream on one side and foam on the other. Garnish with the puffed rice.

corporate pastry chef
Sergio Navarro

www.sushisamba.com

candied peel

Peel of 2 oranges

$\frac{1}{4}$ cup orange juice

1 tablespoon corn syrup

6 tablespoons granulated sugar

figs in port

2 pounds plus 3 ounces fresh figs

4 $\frac{1}{4}$ cups sugar

2 $\frac{1}{2}$ cups port

3 $\frac{1}{4}$ ounces rosella (or red zinger tea)

$\frac{1}{3}$ cup lemon juice

fudge sauce

$\frac{2}{3}$ cup corn syrup

1 $\frac{3}{4}$ cups sugar

$\frac{3}{4}$ cup cocoa powder

$\frac{3}{4}$ cup heavy cream

1 tablespoon butter

$\frac{1}{2}$ cup chopped chocolate

Pinch of salt

1 teaspoon vanilla extract

whipped cream

2 cups heavy cream, heavy

$\frac{1}{4}$ cup powdered sugar

$\frac{1}{8}$ vanilla bean, scraped

chocolate coffee tuile

2 cups (4 sticks) + 2 tablespoons butter

2 cups granulated sugar

2 $\frac{1}{3}$ cups egg whites

4 $\frac{1}{2}$ cups flour

2 cups black cocoa

$\frac{1}{4}$ cup espresso

Crushed espresso beans, as needed

Cocoa nibs, as needed

chocolate espresso cup

YIELDS 60 MINI PORTIONS OR 12 FULL SIZE SERVINGS

Prepare candied peel: Clean the orange peels of pith, cut into 1 $\frac{1}{2}$ x $\frac{1}{2}$" triangles. Rinse orange peels and place in a saucepan. Cover with cold water and bring to a boil. Drain, rinse, return to pan and cover again with fresh cold water. Repeat process 2 more times. Return peels to clean saucepan. Add orange juice, corn syrup, and sugar, covering the peels. Return to heat and simmer for five minutes. Do not boil for too long a period of time as this reduces the liquid too quickly and toughens the peel. Remove from heat, cool and cover well. Refrigerate.

Prepare figs: Bring a large pot of water to a boil. Rinse the figs, then boil for 20 seconds, remove and cool. In a large rondeau, combine sugar, port, rosella, and lemon juice. Bring sugar mixture (syrup), to 225°F. Add figs to syrup, cover with parchment paper and place a lid or plate smaller than the pot inside to weigh the fruit down below the surface. Return liquid to 225°F. Remove from heat, cover and set aside to cool. Remove the figs and slice each one into 6 pieces; reserve chilled. Reduce the fig poaching liquid until syrupy; chill.

Prepare fudge sauce: In large pot, bring corn syrup and 1 cup of water to a boil. In a small bowl, whisk together the sugar and cocoa powder and add to boiling mixture. Boil for ten minutes. Stir in the heavy cream, butter and chocolate, return to a boil. Remove from the heat and add salt and vanilla. Strain.

Prepare whipped cream: Combine the heavy cream, sugar, and scraped vanilla bean in a Pacojet, and process with whipping blade with valve open. You may also use an electric mixer or whip by hand.

Prepare chocolate coffee tuile: Preheat over to 310°F. In an electric mixer fitted with the paddle attachment, whip the butter and sugar until soft and fluffy. Beat in egg whites. Sift the flour, cocoa and espresso together and add to the butter mixture. Using template one-inch circular template, spread on silpat. Sprinkle tuile with crushed espresso beans and cocoa nibs. Bake in oven 4 minutes, or until set.

RECIPE CONTINUES ON PAGE 154

Christopher W. Broberg

pastry chef

10.6 ounces (about 16) egg yolks

¼ cup plus ½ tablespoon sugar

Large pinch of salt

26 ounces soft goat cheese
room temperature

4 ounces cream cheese,
room temperature

14 ounces sour cream or
crème fraîche

sorbet

1 sheet gelatin (optional)

2 ½ cups blood orange juice, divided

1-3 tablespoons sugar

½ cup light corn syrup

1-3 tablespoons Aperol liquor (optional)

Juice of ½ a lemon

phyllo crust

4 sheets phyllo dough,
room temperature

Melted butter

4 tablespoons raw sugar

4 tablespoons finely crushed pistachios

garnish

1 cup shelled pistachio nuts

1 blood orange, segmented

goat's milk cheesecake with blood orange sorbet and sicilian pistachios

YIELDS 40 BITE-SIZED PIECES

Preheat oven to 300°F and position a rack in the center. In a mixing bowl, whisk together the egg yolks, sugar and salt to combine. In another mixing bowl, using a firm spatula or large wooden kitchen spoon, mix together the goat cheese and cream cheese while drizzling in the egg mixture until well combined. Using a spatula, gently fold in sour cream or crème fraîche. Strain the mixture through a fine meshed sieve. Line two 8 x 8 x 1½-inch baking pans with plastic wrap. Divide batter between the 2 pans. Fill the pan ¾ of the way full with cheesecake batter and cover with aluminum foil. Place in the center of a larger baking or roasting pan and pour enough warm water into the larger pan to reach ⅔ of the way up the sides of the smaller pan. Place in the oven and bake for 45 minutes, or until set. Remove from the water bath and refrigerate for at least 4 hours.

Prepare sorbet: Submerge the gelatin sheet in a bowl of cold water for 10 minutes; remove and squeeze out excess water. In a medium sized saucepot over low heat, gently warm 1 cup of the blood orange juice and sugar (1-3 tablespoons depending on the sweetness of the oranges) to just below a simmer. Stir in the gelatin until dissolved. Remove from heat and slowly add the remaining 1½ cups blood orange juice and corn syrup to combine. Transfer the liquid to a bowl or container set over another bowl of ice water, and stir occasionally until well chilled. Taste and adjust flavor with Aperol and lemon juice. Process in an ice cream freezer according to manufacturer's instructions.

Prepare phyllo crust: Preheat oven to 325°F. On a cutting board or other clean flat surface, lay down one sheet of phyllo dough and lightly brush entire surface with melted butter. Evenly sprinkle 1 tablespoon of sugar and 1 tablespoon finely crushed pistachios on top. Repeat process to create four layers. Using a ring mold about the size of a silver dollar, cut out (40) rounds from the layered phyllo. Transfer the phyllo rounds to a parchment paper lined baking sheet and bake for 7 minutes, or until golden brown; cool.

To serve: Toast pistachios at 325°F for 8 minutes or until oily and fragrant. Set aside to cool.Cut out (40) cheesecake rounds with the same cutter the phyllo dough was cut with. Place the cheesecake rounds on top of the phyllo rounds. Place three pistachios on top of each mini cheesecake in the center and a blood orange segment towards the back. Scoop a small amount of blood orange sorbet on top to finish.

ALLEN & DELANCEY

pastry chef

Tiffany MacIsaac

www.allenanddelancey.net

rhubarb chips

1 rhubarb stalk, 1½" in diameter

1 quart grenadine

rhubarb/strawberry sauce

8 rhubarb stalks

1 quart strawberry puree

2 cups orange juice

1 cup sugar plus more to taste

1 vanilla bean, split and scraped

brown butter cake

½ cup brown butter

¾ cup brown sugar, firmly packed

1¼ cups all-purpose flour

1½ teaspoons baking powder

¼ teaspoon salt

¼ cup plus 2 tablespoons cup milk

½ cup egg whites

¼ cup diced rhubarb

pistachio ice cream

1 pint milk

1 pint heavy cream

1 cup sugar, divided

12 egg yolks

1 cup pistachio puree

strawberry mousse

½ cup sugar

¼ cup egg whites

1½ cup strawberry puree

1 tablespoon lemon juice

10.5g gelatin sheets (about 4 sheets)

1¼ cup whipped cream

garnish

Ground Sicilian pistachios

rhubarb brown butter cake with strawberry mousse and pistachio ice cream

YIELDS SIX SERVINGS — ADVANCE PREPARATION REQUIRED

Prepare rhubarb chips: Cut rhubarb stalk in two-inch sections. Using a mandoline, slice the rhubarb pieces lengthwise, until you have 12 strips. Place the strips in a shallow pan. Bring grenadine to a boil and pour it over shaved rhubarb. Cover and let cool to room temperature. Rinse under water and then dry in a dehydrator for 24 hours. Once crisp cut the rectangular chips through the middle diagonally to make 24 chips.

Prepare rhubarb/strawberry sauce: Chop rhubarb in 1-inch pieces. Place all ingredients in a saucepan and simmer until rhubarb falls apart, about 25 to 30 minutes. Puree with a hand or standing blender and adjust sweetness if necessary with sugar. Strain through a fine meshed sieve and cool.

Prepare brown butter cake: Preheat oven to 375°F. In the bowl of an electric mixer fitted with a paddle attachment, combine the butter and sugar until homogeneous. Do not incorporate any air. In a small bowl, combine the flour, baking powder and salt. In another bowl, combine milk and egg whites. In three separate parts: alternate mixing in dry and wet into the butter/sugar mixture. Mix each part until homogenous and stop and scrape the bowl with a rubber spatula three times. Mix in rhubarb dice until just incorporated. Pipe into a 1 x 1 x 2-inch mold. Bake for 15 to 20 minutes.

Prepare pistachio ice cream: In a saucepot, heat the milk, cream and 1/2 cup sugar to scald (just below boiling,) remove from heat. In a separate bowl, combine the egg yolks with the other half of sugar. Temper yolks into milk mixture. Return to the stove and cook until mixture is thick enough to coat the back of a spoon. Whisk in pistachio puree, cool and strain. Process in an ice cream freezer according to manufacturer's instructions.

Prepare mousse: Submerge gelatin sheets in a bowl of cold water for 10 minutes; remove and squeeze out excess water. Make Italian meringue with sugar and whites: In a heavy bottomed pot, add sugar and enough water to form a wet sand like consistency. Start cooking mixture on high heat. Meanwhile, put the whites in a mixer fitted with whisk attachment, turn on high speed when sugar is at 235°F. Once the sugar reaches 240°F stream it down the side of mixing bowl into egg whites with mixer on high speed. Continue to whip until stiff peaks form, about 3 to 5 minutes. Whip the cream to soft peaks. In a heatproof bowl placed on top of a pot of simmering water (without touching the water) combine half of puree and lemon juice, add gelatin; and stir to dissolve. Then, combine in a separate bowl with the other half of puree. Gradually fold meringue into puree mixture. Fold cream into puree/meringue mixture. Transfer to pastry bag. Pipe into (6) 2.5cm cannoli mold; chill.

Plating: Spoon, then streak the sauce onto plate. Place cake in the middle and stand the mousse towards the back of cake. Place the chips in between these two. Add the pistachios next to the mousse and melon ball the ice cream in front of the mousse.

AQUAVIT

pastry chef
Steven Cak

www.aquavit.org

special equipment

Pizzelle Waffle Iron

anise waffle cones

2 ¼ cups all-purpose flour

¼ teaspoon baking powder

5 ounces eggs (3 to 4 eggs)

½ cup sugar

Zest and juice of 1 lemon

1 teaspoon anise extract or
vanilla extract or ground anise

6 tablespoons melted butter

¼ – ½ cup milk

Oil for iron

vanilla ice cream

1 quart milk

4 tablespoons honey

⅓ cup heavy cream

1 vanilla bean, scraped

1 cup sugar, divided

9 egg yolks

1 tablespoon non-fat dry instant
milk powder

vanilla ice cream, anise waffle cones

YIELDS EIGHT SERVINGS

Season Electric Pizzelle iron by brushing with vegetable oil and heating for 10 minutes. Wipe dry.

Prepare anise waffle cones: Sift together flour and baking powder and set aside. In a medium size bowl, beat eggs until frothy (foamy). Add sugar and lemon juice; mix until mixture is light. Add lemon zest and anise. Gradually add the dry ingredients and beat until smooth. Stir in melted butter. Add milk, as needed, for a smooth, runny batter. Lightly brush the iron's surface with oil or non-stick vegetable spray. Heat until a drop of water sizzles. Pour two tablespoons of batter onto one side. Close iron and scrape off excess batter, if any, from the edges. Cook until golden brown. While still hot, quickly roll the waffle around a cone-shaped mold, sealing the point. Remove from the mold when cool. Repeat with remaining batter.

Prepare ice cream: In a saucepot, combine the milk, honey, heavy cream, vanilla bean, and 1/2 cup sugar, and bring to a boil. In a mixing bowl, combine the remaining 1/2 cup sugar with egg yolks; whisk for one minute to aerate. Add powdered milk. Slowly stream the boiling milk over egg yolk mixture while whisking, until combined. Return the mixture to the pot and cook over medium heat, whisking, until the mixture reaches 185°F. Remove from heat and strain the mixture through a fine meshed sieve into a medium bowl set over another bowl of ice water; stir occasionally until well chilled. Process in an ice cream machine according to the manufacturer's instructions. Keep in freezer until desired consistency.

Bill Yosses

pastry chef

strawberry cheesecake with roasted pineapple

small things SWEET

graham cracker crumb crust

7 tablespoons unsalted butter, melted, divided

1 cup graham cracker crumbs

¼ cup granulated sugar

cheesecake batter

1½ pounds cream cheese, at room temperature

6 tablespoons unsalted butter, at room temperature

1 cup granulated sugar

3 tablespoons cornstarch

1 cup sour cream

¼ cup cream sherry or sweet Marsala

2 teaspoons vanilla extract

4 large eggs

garnish

Pineapple

Sliced strawberries

Prepare graham cracker crust: Preheat the oven to 350°F and position a rack in the center. Brush an 8-inch springform pan or an 8-inch cake pan with 1 tablespoon of the melted butter. If you're using a springform pan, wrap the outside with aluminum foil. Combine the graham cracker crumbs and sugar in a medium bowl. Add remaining 6 tablespoons of melted butter and mix thoroughly. Pat the mixture evenly onto the bottom of the prepared cake pan. Bake for 7 minutes, or until lightly colored at the edges. Cool at room temperature while preparing the filling.

Prepare batter: Set a rack in the bottom third of the oven and reduce the oven temperature to 300°F. Put the cream cheese, butter, sugar, and cornstarch in a large mixing bowl and beat with an electric mixer at medium speed until just blended (take care not to mix too much air into batter). Beat in the sour cream, sherry and vanilla. Add eggs one at a time, beating in-between additions to incorporate well. Pour the batter into prepared cake pan with the graham cracker crust. Place the cake pan in a large roasting pan and pour enough hot water into the roasting pan to come about 1 inch up the sides of the cake pan. Cover the roasting pan with foil and bake for 1 hour. Remove foil and bake for 15 to 30 minutes, until very lightly tanned, slightly puffed and barely firm. Remove from oven and cool to room temperature in a water bath. Remove from bath and refrigerate overnight.

Prepare roasted pineapple: Preheat the oven to 350°F. Place on a silpat lines cookie sheet and lightly spray with vegetable oil. Peel and core the pineapple. Cut into bite-sized pieces and place on the silpat. Bake for 15 minutes, until barely browned. Let cool.

Assembly: To release the cake, place into a 350°F oven for 2 minutes. If using a springform pan, snap the catch to release the sides. For a regular pan, invert onto a plate covered with plastic wrap or foil. Give a shake to release. Now turn right side up onto a serving platter and peel off the foil or plastic. If needed, run a thin knife blade around the sides of the cake to help loosen.

When completely chilled, horizontally slice the cheesecake through the middle. Cut the top and bottom layers into 1-inch triangles. Group a few slices of strawberries on each plate. Top with one piece of cheesecake with the crust, follow with a slice of strawberry then another piece of cake and strawberry slice. Top with 2 pieces of roasted pineapple. Decorate plates with fruit coulis or puree.

PORTER HOUSE
NEW YORK

executive pastry chef

Wayne Brachman

www.porterhousenewyork.com

carrot cake

2 ½ cups rice flour

2 cups sugar

1¼ cups vegetable oil (or preferred)

½ cup milk

2 teaspoons baking powder

2 teaspoons cinnamon

1 teaspoon baking soda

½ teaspoon salt

4 eggs

4 cups carrots, grated

1 cup chopped nuts or raisins (optional)

mascarpone mousse

¾ cup heavy cream, whipped

2 sheets gelatin

3 egg yolks

6 tablespoons sugar

¼ cup white wine mixed with
2 tablespoons vanilla extract

1 cup mascarpone cheese

roasted walnut ice cream

1½ cups walnut halves or pieces

1 quart milk

1 cup sugar

12 egg yolks

1 vanilla bean, cut in half lengthwise

walnut nougatine

1 pound sugar

1 teaspoon lemon juice

1½ cups walnut pieces

garnish

3 freshly grated and squeezed carrots

gluten-free carrot cake with mascarpone mousse

YIELDS 12 SERVINGS — ADVANCE PREPARATION REQUIRED

Prepare carrot cake: Wash carrots, trim off stems and grate. Set aside until batter is mixed. If using nuts or raisins, set aside as well. Preheat oven to 350°F. In the bowl of an electric mixer fitted with the paddle attachment, combine all other ingredients and mix 5 to 7 minutes on low speed. Scrape the bowl and paddle with a spatula once or twice during mixing. Stir in the carrots, and nuts or raisins if using, and pour batter into either a 10-inch round cake pan or a 13 x 18 x 1" baking pan, sprayed with non-stick cooking spray and lined with parchment paper. Bake until well risen, and a knife or skewer inserted in the center comes out clean, approximately 25 to 30 minutes. Set aside to cool completely before icing.

Prepare mascarpone mousse: In the bowl of an electric mixer fitted with the whisk attachment, whip the cream until soft peaks form. Refrigerate until needed. Soften gelatin sheets in a bowl of cold water for 10 minutes; squeeze out excess liquid. Combine the egg yolks, sugar, wine, and vanilla mixture in a medium heat-proof bowl and place over a pot of simmering water (being sure the bottom of the bowl does not touch the water); whip until thickened and pale. Remove from heat and continue whipping with electric mixer until cold and increased in volume. Meanwhile, place drained gelatin in a small metal bowl over the simmering water, to melt. Remove a spatula-full of the egg mixture and fold into dissolved gelatin. Fold this mixture back into the egg mix. Soften mascarpone cheese with a rubber spatula and fold into egg mixture. Fold in softly whipped cream.

Assemble cake: Slice the cooled carrot cake in half horizontally and spread mascarpone mousse on top of each piece. Stack back together and refrigerate several hours before cutting 3 x 1½ inch rectangles.

Prepare roasted walnut ice cream: Arrange walnut pieces on a baking tray, and toast in a 325°F oven, for 15 minutes, or until walnuts are fragrant and lightly toasted. Remove from oven and put in a saucepan with milk, sugar, and vanilla bean. Heat mixture to a boil, and turn off heat, covering pot with a lid. Allow walnuts and vanilla to steep in milk 20 to 30 minutes. Strain out walnuts and vanilla, and discard. Meanwhile, gently whisk egg yolks in a medium bowl. Reheat milk and sugar to the boil. Gently and slowly, whisk hot milk into egg yolks, whisking the entire time. Return entire mixture to the saucepan, and whisk over medium heat 15 to 30 seconds, or until mixture reaches 182°F. Immediately pour mixture into a bowl placed in another bowl of ice water. Allow mixture to cool, stirring occasionally, then refrigerate overnight.
The next day, process in an ice cream machine according to the manufacturer's instructions.

RECIPE CONTINUES ON PAGE 154

The Institute
of Culinary Education

chef' instructor - director,
center for advanced pastry studies

Michelle Tampakis

www.iceculinary.com

chocolate truffles

YIELDS 30 PIECES — ADVANCE PREPARATION REQUIRED

1 cup heavy cream

2 tablespoons sweet butter

4 tablespoons sugar

1 pound semi sweet chocolate
(chips or chopped)

In a medium heavy-bottom saucepan, combine the heavy cream, butter, and sugar. Bring to a simmer, stirring and add the chocolate. Lower the heat, and stir until melted and smooth. The flavors of Grand Marnier, Sambuca, nuts of your choice can be added to the mixture. Remove from heat, cover lightly, and let sit for two hours. For the best results, let sit overnight at room temperature.

Place the chocolate mixture in the bowl of an electric mixer fitted with a paddle attachment, whip until smooth. Transfer to a pastry bag. Line a baking sheet with waxed paper and pipe the truffle mixture into one-inch balls. Roll the balls in the palms of your hands to make a perfect sphere. If desired, dip into chocolate glaze* and set in the refrigerator for a shiny finish.

* AVAILABLE AT PARISGOURMET.COM

small things SWEET

pastry chef
Claudio Quito

www.tamarinde22.com

baba

2 cups bread flour

¼ teaspoon salt

2 teaspoons fresh yeast

1 teaspoon honey

¼ cup butter, room temperature

5 eggs

raspberry juice

2 pounds raspberries

2 cups sugar

Peel of 1 orange

Peels of 2 lemons

½ vanilla pod, skin only

raspberry sauce

1 pound raspberries

½ cup sugar, divided

½ teaspoon apple pectin

lemon thyme gelée

6 springs lemon thyme

½ vanilla bean, scraped

1¼ cups sugar

5 sheets gelatin

½ cup lemon juice

whipped crème fraîche

1 cup crème fraîche

1 cup heavy cream

½ cup sugar

½ teaspoon vanilla extract

garnish

Apricot nappage (apricot glaze or jelly)

Fresh raspberries, slice in half

Fresh leaves of lemon thyme

raspberry baba with lemon thyme gelée and whipped crème fraîche

YIELDS 24 SMALL BABAS — ADVANCE PREPARATION REQUIRED

Prepare baba: Preheat oven to 400°F. In the bowl of an electric mixer fitted with the dough hook attachment, mix in order listed the flour, salt, yeast, honey, butter, then eggs, until well combined. Pour into an oiled bowl and cover for one hour at room temperature to allow proofing. Transfer dough into a piping bag fitted with a round tip and pipe into 24 – 1/2 wide x 2" high greased ring molds set on top of a parchment paper lined baking sheet 3/4 of the way full. Cover with plastic and proof again. Remove plastic when dough rises close to the top. Bake 12-15 minutes or until golden brown and cooked through. Carefully remove from molds while still hot and set aside at room temperature to cool. Store covered at room temperature.

Prepare raspberry juice: Combine the raspberries, 8 cups water, sugar, peels, and vanilla pod in a pot and bring to a boil over medium heat. Remove from heat, cover, and set aside to cool. Strain through a fine meshed sieve and reserve for soaking the babas.

Prepare raspberry sauce: Mix the raspberries with 1/4 cup of the sugar in a stainless steel bowl. Wrap tightly with plastic wrap. Place over a pot of lightly simmering water (without the bowl touching the water) for 2 hours. Strain through a fine meshed sieve. Scale 2 cups of the liquid and discard remaining juice. In a small bowl, mix the remaining 1/4 cup sugar with the pectin. Boil the juice and slowly whisk in the pectin sugar. Strain and cool.

Prepare gelée: Submerge the gelatin sheets in a bowl of cold water for 10 minutes; remove and squeeze out excess water. In a medium saucepot, bring the lemon thyme, vanilla bean, 4 cups water and sugar to a boil. Remove from heat, stir in the gelatin until dissolved. Cover and set aside to cool to room temperature. Stir in thr lemon juice, strain through a fine meshed sieve into a shallow baking dish and let set overnight. The following day, cut the gelée into 1/4" cubes.

Prepare whipped crème fraîche: Whip together the crème fraîche, cream, sugar and vanilla extract until stiff peaks form. Chill until ready to use.

To serve: Soak the cooled babas in warmed raspberry juice, 3-5 minutes. Strain on a baking rack. Brush with warmed apricot nappage. Refrigerate. Drag a line of raspberry sauce across each plate diagonally. Place one baba centered across the sauce line. Put a quenelle of whipped crème fraîche next to the baba. Garnish plates with sliced raspberries, cubes of lemon thyme gelée, and lemon thyme leaves.

executive pastry chef

Jansen Chan

www.oceanarestaurant.com

pistachio financier

5 ½ cups pistachio flour

2 ¾ cups pastry or cake flour

4 ½ cups granulated sugar

2 tablespoons kosher salt

2 cups (16 oz) browned butter, melted

13 egg whites

¼ cup orange blossom honey

Zest of 1 orange

1 tablespoon vanilla extract

2 teaspoons orange blossom water

kumquat coulis

8 ounces (about 2 cups) kumquats, halved, seeded, and blanched 3 times

1 cup orange juice

¼ cup dry white wine

¾ cup granulated sugar

¼ cup orange blossom honey

Salt

2 tablespoons Cointreau

orange blossom foam

1 cup skim milk

½ teaspoon salt

1 tablespoon soy lecithin granules

2 tablespoons orange blossom honey

1 tablespoon Cointreau

1 teaspoon orange blossom water

garnish

Candied pistachios (optional)

Candied kumquats (optional)

pistachio financier with candied kumquats and orange blossom foam

YIELDS 48 SERVINGS — 1x1 INCH CUBES

Prepare pistachio financier: Preheat oven to 350°F. In a mixing bowl of a KitchenAid or a stand mixer fitted with a whisk attachment, combine the flours, sugar, and salt. Stream in the egg whites on low speed. Scrape the sides and bottom of bowl with a rubber spatula, then add the honey. Still on low speed, stream in the melted brown butter, vanilla and orange blossom water. Once all is incorporated, change to medium speed and mix for 30 seconds. Allow the batter to chill for at least an hour. Bake in greased one-inch cubed silicon molds until golden brown and springs back upon touching, about 20 minutes.

Prepare kumquat coulis: In a medium heavy saucepan, combine the blanched kumquats with the orange juice, white wine, sugar, and honey. Bring to a boil, then reduce to a simmer and cook, stirring occasionally, for 30 to 45 minutes, until the liquid reduces to half and the kumquats are translucent. Allow mixture to cool to room temperature. Transfer to a powerful blender and puree until smooth. Strain the mixture through a fine meshed sieve. Finish the sauce with a touch of salt and the Cointreau.

Prepare orange blossom foam: Combine all ingredients in a small saucepot, and heat through to dissolve the seasonings. When ready to serve, "buzz" with a hand-held blender until a foam is created, about 10 seconds.

Plating: Garnish the bottom of up to 48 serving plates with a swirl of the kumquat coulis. Place a piece of financier on the plate, then top with a spoonful of orange blossom foam. Garnish with candied pistachios and kumquats.

BOKA

pastry chef
Elizabeth Dahl

www.bokachicago.com

chambord gelée

¼ cup grenadine

¾ cup plus 1 tablespoon Chambord

1¼ cups water

⅔ cup sugar

1 tablespoon plus 1 teaspoon NH pectin

1¾ teaspoons citric acid

mandarin gelée

2 cups mandarin puree

1⅓ cup sugar

1 tablespoon plus 1 teaspoon NH pectin

1¾ teaspoons citric acid

crispy vanilla bean

Vanilla beans

Simple syrup

mandarin curd

3 egg yolks

¼ cup sugar

¼ cup mandarin orange juice

1 teaspoon lemon juice

garnish

Freeze-dried raspberry powder*

Fresh raspberries, halved

*AVAILABLE AT WHOLE FOODS UNDER THE BRAND NAME
JUST RASPBERRIES OR ONLINE AT LEPICERIE.COM

mandarin & chambord gelée with raspberry and crispy vanilla bean

YIELDS 50 SMALL BITES — ADVANCE PREPARATION REQUIRED

Prepare each gelée separately as follows: Put the liquids in a pot; combine the dry ingredients and whisk into the liquid. Bring to a boil and simmer for 1 minute, remove from heat. Cool at room temperature for 5 minutes then strain into a flat pan lined with plastic wrap. Set aside to reach room temperature; then refrigerate at least 2 hours. Cut to uniform sizes and keep refrigerated.

Prepare vanilla bean: Use leftover (already scraped) vanilla beans if available. Julienne into fine strips. Place in pot and cover with simple syrup. Simmer for one hour or until soft. Drain, separate, and dehydrate (or place in a barely warm oven) overnight.

Prepare mandarin curd: Whisk all ingredients in a heatproof bowl over a pot of simmering water (being sure that the bottom of the bowl does not touch the water), until thickened. Strain and cool in an ice bath.

To serve: Stack one piece of Chambord gelée directly on top of a piece of the mandarin. Sprinkle the gelées and a bit of the plate with raspberry powder. Garnish with a half a fresh raspberry and a couple strips of the crispy vanilla bean. Finish by dotting plate with mandarin curd.

T R U

pastry chef
Meg Galus

www.trurestaurant.com

chocolate-covered cornflakes

YIELDS ABOUT SIX DOZEN PIECES

4 cups cornflakes (or other similar cereal)

16 ounces bittersweet chocolate, chopped

Place the bittersweet chocolate in a heatproof bowl over a pot of simmering water (being sure that the bottom of the bowl does not touch the water), and heat, stirring occasionally to form a smooth slightly thickened liquid. The chocolate should be warmer than body temperature, but not hot. If the chocolate is too hot, set aside for 5 or 10 minutes to cool.

Place the cornflakes in a large mixing bowl. Add about half of the warm chocolate. Use a rubber spatula to mix the two together until cornflakes are evenly coated. Let sit for a minute or two and then repeat with the remaining warm chocolate.

With two large spoons, quickly scoop the chocolate-covered cornflakes into small mounds onto wax or parchment paper covered baking sheets; using one spoon to scoop the mixture from the bowl and the other to scrape the mixture onto the baking sheet. Work quickly as the chocolate may begin to set and harden before all of the scoops are completed.

If the chocolate is not fully set once all of the mixture is scooped into mounds, place in the refrigerator to harden for 5 to 10 minutes. Store the chocolate cornflakes in an airtight container in a cool, dry area. They will keep for 2 weeks.

small things SWEET

chef - owner

Jacques Torres

www.mrchocolate.com

the french cone

YIELDS APPROXIMATELY 40 CONES

raspberry tuile

4 ¾ ounces powdered sugar

1 ¼ ounces flour

1 ¾ ounces butter, softened

1 ¼ ounces raspberry puree (warmed)

concord grape sorbet

3 cups Concord grapes

2 tablespoons sugar

Juice of 1 large lemon

½ cup simple syrup

fromage blanc sorbet syrup

1 ¼ cups sugar

1 ½ cups water

½ cup glucose syrup

fromage blanc sorbet

24 ounces fromage blanc

1 ¼ cups Sorbet Syrup (recipe above)

1 cup lime juice

Chefs note: The frog is a pulled sugar decoration, and inspiration for the name of the dessert.

Prepare raspberry tuile: Preheat oven to 325°F. Pass the sugar and flour through a fine meshed sieve into separate bowls. In an electric mixer fitted with a paddle attachment, cream the butter and sugar until smooth; pour in puree. Add the flour and mix until well combined. Spread batter onto a silpat-lined baking sheet using a circular mold as a template (use a 3" diameter circular template - you will fit approximately 12 per baking sheet). Bake for 10 minutes. While still warm, fold over cone and reserve. Hold in a dry air-tight container until ready to use. Continue this process until all of the batter is used.

Prepare grape sorbet: Blend grapes with sugar and lemon juice and bring to a boil. Strain through chinois or fine mesh strainer. Pour in simple syrup and chill. Process in an ice cream freezer according to the manufacturer's instructions.

Prepare fromage blanc sorbet syrup: Bring sugar, water and glucose syrup to a boil in a medium pot. Cool to room temperature.

Prepare fromage blanc sorbet: Mix the fromage blanc, Sorbet Syrup, and lime juice together. Process in an ice cream freezer according to the manufacturer's instructions.

small things SWEET

executive pastry chef
Marc Aumont

pastry chef
Patrick Clark

www.themodernnyc.com

½ pound silken tofu

1 pound cream cheese

½ pound sour cream

¼ pound white miso

1⅔ cups sugar

1 pound + 10 ounces sweet potato, pureed, roasted

½ cup kuzu root starch

1½ cups organic soy milk

6 large eggs

crust

3 cups graham cracker crumbs

½ cup (1 stick) butter

1 tablespoon white miso

3 tablespoons sugar

milk chocolate mousse

1 pound + 11 oz milk chocolate, chopped

3¼ cups heavy cream

1½ cups organic soy milk

2 tablespoons sugar

2 tablespoons vanilla paste

⅓ cup egg yolk

cocoa nib tuile

1 cup sugar

¼ cup isomalt

¼ cup glucose

⅓ cup water

⅓ cocoa nibs

garnish

Kuromitsu (Japanese black sugar syrup), or substitute maple syrup or honey

small things SWEET

sweet potato tofu cheesecake

YIELDS EIGHT SERVINGS — ADVANCE PREPARATION REQUIRED

Prepare crust: In a small bowl, combine the graham cracker crumbs, melted butter, white miso, and sugar. Press mixture firmly onto the bottom of a 12 x 12-inch springform pan. Set aside.

Prepare cheesecake: Preheat oven to 350°F. In the bowl of an electric mixer fitted with a paddle attachment, combine the tofu, cream cheese, and sour cream; mix until smooth. Add the white miso, sugar, and pureed roasted sweet potato and mix until smooth. In a small pot, scald the soy milk. Whisk the kuzu into very warm soy milk until completely dissolved. Let the soy milk cool to room temperature and then add to the tofu mix. Add the eggs one at a time, completely mixing in-between each addition. Pour mixture into prepared crust and bake in oven for about one hour or until set.

Prepare mousse: Put the chocolate in a heatproof bowl. Bring a small pot filled 1/3 with water to a simmer and place the bowl on top (without touching the water). Stir the chocolate with a wooden spoon until melted. Remove from heat and cool to just above room temperature. In a chilled metal bowl, beat the heavy cream until it begins to thicken. Add in organic soy milk, sugar and vanilla paste, continuing to whip. Beat egg yolks until light and airy, gradually fold them into the melted chocolate. Next, gently fold in soy milk heavy cream mixture into the chocolate. Chill the mousse several hours or overnight.

Prepare cocoa nib tuile: Combine sugar, isomalt, glucose, and water in a pot; heat to 300°F. Immediately remove from heat and let cool for one minute. Blend in cocoa nibs. Pour mixture onto a silpat and let harden. Once hardened, blend in food processor until it forms a powder. Cut a 1-inch round stencil (you can use anything firm, an old milk carton for example). Place stencil on clean silpat. Dust powder over stencil until surface area is covered. Bake at 350°F until crisp, approximately 3 minutes. Yields approximately 50 tuiles.

Assembly: Before serving, remove sides of springform pan. Cut the cheesecake in 1.5 x 1.5-inch squares. Top each square with a scoop of the milk chocolate mousse and a cocoa nib tuile. Brush some kuromitsu on the bottom of a plate and top with a piece of cheesecake.

chef-owner
Michael Berl

www.kyotofu-nyc.com

pain perdue custard

3 cups heavy cream

1 cup milk

½ cup plus 2 tablespoons sugar

2 vanilla beans, scraped

9 egg yolks

strawberry and rhubarb jam

2 cups roughly chopped rhubarb

½ cup sugar

2 cups roughly chopped strawberries

rhubarb chips

2 cups sugar

2 cups water

2 stalks of rhubarb, cut to 6" pieces

strawberry dice

6 strawberries, rinsed

1 tablespoon sugar

Squeeze of lemon juice

brioche

⅛ cup sugar

1 tablespoon fresh yeast

4 eggs

¼ cup milk

1¼ cups flour

3 cups butter, soft

ginger crème fraîche

1 cup crème fraîche

½ cup sugar

2 tablespoons fresh grated ginger

pain perdue with ginger crème fraîche, fresh strawberries & strawberry & rhubarb jam

YIELDS SIX SERVINGS — ADVANCE PREPARATION REQUIRED

Prepare pain perdue : In a medium size pot, combine heavy cream, milk, sugar and vanilla and heat to a simmer. Remove from heat transfer to a bowl placed over another bowl of ice water to chill. Whisk in the egg yolks, then strain through a fine meshed sieve. Refrigerate until ready to use.

Prepare strawberry and rhubarb jam: Place the rhubarb and sugar into a medium heavy-bottom pot over low heat. Cook, stirring occasionally, for 15 to 20 minutes; or until the rhubarb breaks down. Add strawberries and cook, stirring occasionally, 20 to 25 minutes, or until strawberry and rhubarb breaks down well and thickens; remove from heat and cool at room temperature. Cover and reserve chilled until ready to use.

Prepare rhubarb chips: Preheat oven to 100°F. Combine water and sugar in a pot and simmer for 5 minutes. Using a mandoline, slice the rhubarb pieces lengthwise, until you have 6 to 7 strips per piece. Place strips into warm sugar syrup and simmer for 2 to 3 minutes. Strain the rhubarb and pat dry. Lay the rhubarb strips flat onto a silpat-lined baking sheet. Bake for 30 to 40 minutes, or until the chips are dry but not colored. When the rhubarb chips are still warm, remove them with an offset spatula, and using your fingers, bend into decorative curls.

Prepare strawberry dice: Cut the strawberries in to slices, then into small dice, add the sugar and a squeeze of lemon juice. Reserve until plating.

Prepare brioche: In the bowl of an electric mixer fitted with the whisk attachment, whip sugar, yeast, eggs, and milk until combined. Add flour, and mix with a dough hook until a dough forms, about 4 to 5 minutes. Gradually add soft butter, completely blending in-between each addition, until all of the butter is incorporated. Mix for another 4 to 5 minutes on medium speed. Transfer dough to a covered bowl and refrigerate overnight. The next day, preheat oven to 350°F and place a rack in the center. Place dough in a greased and floured 6 by 4-inch loaf pan, cover and set in a warm place for 45 to 60 minutes, once dough doubles in size, bake for 45 minutes until brioche is done.

Prepare ginger crème fraîche: Whip together the crème fraîche, sugar and ginger until stiff peaks form. Keep chilled until ready to use.

Prepare pain perdue: Cut the brioche into 1½ x ¼" thick squares. Soak brioche squares in Pain Perdue Custard for 10 to 12 minutes. In a medium skillet, heat butter and brown brioche on both sides. Drain on paper towels.

To serve: Drag a spoonful of strawberry rhubarb jam across each plate diagonally. Place one pain perdue square in center. Using a hot espresso spoon, shape the crème fraîche into 6 ovals. Place one crème fraîche oval on the left side of the pain perdue. Put a teaspoon full of diced strawberries to the side of oval. Garnish with rhubarb chip and micro shiso.

pastry chef

Ken Larsen

www.patinagroup.com

vahlrona pudding cake

2 cups granulated sugar + extra for dusting

¾ cup honey tangerine juice

10 ounces Vahlrona chocolate, bittersweet

1½ cups unsalted butter, room temperature, diced, plus extra for greasing cups

8 eggs

⅔ cup Banana-Date Puree (recipe follows)

2 ¾ tablespoon all-purpose flour

Pinch of salt

banana-date puree

11 large bananas, reserve 1 for garnish

1 quart Medjool dates

Salt

chili-spiked tangerine sauce

1 quart juice from honey tangerines

1 vanilla bean

¼ cup sugar

1 Thai chili pepper (optional)

2 tablespoons arrowroot

3 tablespoons water

Pinch of salt

dried banana date chip

1 cup Banana-Date Puree (recipe above)

garnish

Honey tangerines

chocolate pudding cake with chili-tangerine sauce

YIELDS TWENTY SERVINGS

Prepare Vahlrona pudding cake: Preheat oven to 325°F. Lightly butter 4-ounce cups and dust with sugar. Mix sugar and tangerine juice in pot, bring to a boil. Pour over chocolate and mix until dissolved. Add diced butter until dissolved. Next, gradually add the eggs (beaten). Add Banana Date Puree and mix well. Add the flour and salt. Pour mixture into molds, filling to the rim. Place molds in a shallow pan and pour in enough hot water to reach half the height of the pan. Bake for 12 to 15 minutes until the cake forms a thin, dry crust. Drain off water; cool at room temperature then refrigerate.

Prepare banana-date puree: Preheat the oven to 325°F. Arrange ten large, ripened bananas on parchment paper lined sheet tray lined. Pierce the bananas with a paring knife to avoid bursting. Roast in the oven until soft and black, approximately 20 minutes. Let cool.
Bring a large pot of lightly salted water to a boil and place a bowl of ice water on the side. Add one quart of whole Medjool dates to pot and boil for approximately four minutes. Remove dates and chill in the ice water. Using a paring knife, skin the dates and slice in half, removing pits and stems. (Reserve five presentable halves for garnish.) Combine dates and bananas in a food processor and puree until smooth.

Prepare tangerine sauce: In a heavy, two-quart saucepot, bring tangerine juice, vanilla bean, sugar, salt and chili pepper to a boil. Place a bowl of ice water on the side. Whisk arrowroot and water together to produce a thin paste. As juice comes to a boil, add the arrowroot mixture while whisking rapidly for 30 seconds. Strain into a container and set over the bowl of ice water. Let cool. Taste and adjust for sweetness, spiciness and texture. To adjust, either add more sugar, steep chili pepper longer, or add more tangerine juice.

Prepare dried banana date chip: Preheat oven to 200°F. Using an offset spatula, and a plastic rectangular stencil spread even strips of puree onto on a flat sheet tray that's lined with silicon baking mat. Dry in the oven until pliable. Remove from mat and store in a dry, airtight container.

Prepare garnish: Using a sharp knife, segment the honey tangerines, discarding the seeds. Slice the dates and bananas into sizes similar to the honey tangerines. Toss all fruit together in the reserved juice.

Assembly: Unmold cake onto plate, placing it slightly off-center on a small plate. Place banana date chip atop cake, and arrange the fruit garnish on top of the chip. Spoon tangerine sauce on the plate in a decorative fashion.

ROUGE TOMATE restaurant

executive pastry sous chef

Rob Valencia

www.rougetomatenyc.com

scones

4 ¼ cups all-purpose flour

¼ cup sugar plus extra for dusting

2 tablespoons baking powder

2 teaspoons salt

1 tablespoon orange zest

¾ pound unsalted butter, cold

4 eggs, lightly beaten

1 cup buttermilk, cold

1 egg, beaten, for egg wash

shortcake

1 pint strawberries, rinsed

1 cup canned lychee, cut in quarters

1 teaspoon orange zest

2 tablespoons powdered sugar

8 mint leaves, chiffonade (sliced thinly)

4 tablespoons balsamic glaze* or aged balsamic vinegar

2 cups whipped cream

* AVAILABLE AT ITALIAN SPECIALTY STORES

strawberry lychee shortcake

YIELDS SIX SERVINGS

Prepare scones: Sift all the dry ingredients together. Preheat oven to 400°F. In the bowl of an electric mixer fitted with a paddle attachment, add flour, sugar, baking powder, salt, and orange zest. Add the butter and mix on low until the batter is the size of peas. Combine eggs and buttermilk together. Add the liquid to the dry ingredients slowly in a steady stream. Mix until just blended, add additional flour to adjust consistency if needed, wrap in plastic and chill in the refrigerator. Roll out dough on a flat, floured surface until 3/4-inch thick. Cut dough with ring cutter to desired size or shape. Brush with egg wash, sprinkle with sugar and bake for 20 to 25 minutes until tops are browned.

Prepare fruit filling: Hull strawberries and cut into quarters. Cut lychees into quarters and toss with strawberries, orange zest and sugar. Slice the scones in half lengthwise and top with strawberry-lychee compote, then top with whipped cream. Garnish shortcakes with mint chiffonade, and then drizzle balsamic glaze and remaining juices from fruit compote.

A USTA EVENT

executive chef

Michael Lockard

www.levyrestaurants.com

2 cups heavy whipping cream

3 egg yolks

3 tablespoons instant espresso powder
(preferably Medaglia D'oro)

½ cup sugar, divided

3 egg whites

espresso-almond shortbread (10 to 12)

¼ pound unsalted butter

¼ cup sugar

1 teaspoon vanilla extract

1 large egg

⅔ cup all-purpose flour

½ cup almond flour

1 tablespoon ground espresso

Pinch of salt

salted caramel sauce (2 cups)

2 tablespoons water

2 tablespoons corn syrup

½ pound sugar

1 cup heavy cream

1 teaspoon sea salt

almond nougatine (12 to 15)

2 tablespoons sugar

2 tablespoons butter

2 tablespoons light corn syrup

2 tablespoons all-purpose flour

Pinch of salt

4 tablespoons coarsely chopped almonds

espresso semifreddo, espresso-almond shortbread, sea salt caramel sauce & almond nougatine

YIELDS TEN SERVINGS — ADVANCE PREPARATION REQUIRED

Prepare semifreddo: Whip heavy cream to medium peaks and set aside in the refrigerator. In a the bowl of a stand mixer fit with a whip attachment, combine the yolks, espresso powder, and 1/4 cup sugar, and mix on high speed until thick, glossy and about doubled in volume. Transfer mixture into a large mixing bowl; set aside. In the bowl of a stand mixer, combine egg whites and remaining sugar and place over a pot of simmering water (being sure the bottom of the bowl does not touch the water). Gently whisk until mixture reaches 140°F. Immediately transfer the bowl to a mixer fitted with the whip attachment and whip until about doubled in volume. Using a large rubber spatula, fold the egg whites into the yolk mixture. Then fold the whipped cream into mixture until evenly incorporated and smooth. Spoon mixture into 10 – 4 ounce ramekins or a terrine mold and freeze for four hours to overnight.

Prepare shortbread: In the bowl of a stand mixer fitted with the paddle attachment, cream the butter and sugar together on medium speed, until light and fluffy. Add the vanilla extract and egg and mix until well incorporated. Slowly add the all-purpose flour, almond flour, espresso and salt. Mix until well incorporated. Turn the dough out onto a large piece of parchment paper, top with another piece of parchment and roll until the dough is 1/4-inch thick. Transfer to a baking sheet, remove top layer of parchment paper, and score with a 3-inch round cookie cutter. Cover sheet with plastic wrap and freeze dough for 2 hours to one week.

When ready to bake, preheat the oven to 325°F. Pop out rounds of frozen dough and place on a parchment lined cookie sheet, about 1-inch apart. Bake for approximately 8 to 12 minutes, until light golden brown. Set aside to cool at room temperature.

RECIPE CONTINUES ON PAGE 154

pastry chef

Jenny McCoy

www.avocerestaurant.com

chocolate beignet

dough

¼ cup butter

½ cup cream cheese

1 cup all-purpose flour

½ teaspoon salt

½ teaspoon baking powder

filling

1 cup chocolate, chopped

⅓ cup heavy cream

2 tablespoons butter

to assemble

1 egg, beaten (egg wash)

Oil, as needed for frying

Powdered sugar

Prepare dough: Beat the butter and cream cheese until well combined. Sift the flour, salt and baking powder together and combine with the butter-cream cheese mixture. Wrap the dough in plastic tightly and chill at least 30 minutes.

Prepare filling: Place the chopped chocolate, heavy cream and butter in a heat-proof bowl over a pot of simmering water (being sure that the bottom of bowl does not touch the water), and heat, stirring occasionally to form a smooth slightly thickened liquid. Chill until firm enough to scoop.

Assembly: Roll dough on a surface lightly dusted with flour to 1/4 inch thick into. Cut dough in half and brush one half with egg wash. Cut each half into (10) 2-inch squares and place 1 teaspoon of chocolate in middle of the 10 squares that have been brushed with egg wash. Cover the pieces with the other 10 squares and seal the edges with a fork (like a ravioli). Fill a large pot 1/3 full with frying oil and heat to 350°F. Deep-fry the beignet in two batches, draining onto a paper towel lined plate. Dust with powdered sugar and serve warm.

LANDMARC

pastry chef
Regina Anderson

www.landmarc-restaurant.com

Prepare rhubarb: Preheat oven to 300°F. Wash and trim off the ends of the rhubarb. Slice each rib of rhubarb in half, lengthwise. Slice each length on a bias into 1-inch batons, toss with sugar in a bowl and cover with plastic wrap, allowing them to macerate for at least 1/2 hour at room temperature. Place batons of rhubarb on a greased cookie sheet (reserve liquid left in bowl). Bake the rhubarb for about 20 to 30 minutes, until soft and tender but holding its shape. Do not allow it to brown. Drizzle the reserved liquid over the cooked rhubarb and set aside to cool to room temperature.

Prepare candied kumquat: Trim and discard the stem and bottom ends of the kumquats. Slice remaining kumquat into 3 to 5 slices, (about 1/16" thick) depending on size. Place sliced kumquats in a small pot with sugar, 3 tablespoons water, and corn syrup and bring fruit to a simmer. Simmer slowly, stirring once or twice, 6 to10 minutes, until kumquats become translucent. Remove the pot from heat and set aside to cool kumquats in the syrup. These kumquats keep in their syrup for several weeks in the refrigerator.

Prepare rhubarb chips: Cut the rhubarb into 5" cross-sections. Slice the sections lengthwise, as thinly as possible on a mandolin or deli slicer. Toss the rhubarb with the sugar, cover and rest for 45 minutes. Flatten out each slice of rhubarb on silicon mats and bake them in a 200°F oven for 1/2 hour. Peel off the dried rhubarb sticks immediately upon removing the trays from the oven.

Prepare coconut tuile cones: In a stainless steel bowl over simmering water whisk together the egg whites and granulated sugar until the sugar has dissolved and the egg whites are luke warm. With a whisk, gently and thoroughly mix in the flour and salt. Slowly drizzle the warm coconut oil into the batter while whisking; chill.

Preheat oven to 325°F. Using a circular stencil (size based on the size cone you are using to form); thinly spread the batter onto a silpat-lined baking sheet. Bake until golden brown, about 10 minutes. Remove from the oven and while still warm, wrap cookies around a small cone shaped instrument. Allow the tuiles to cool a bit and harden on the form before sliding them off.

Assembly: Spoon some rice pudding into cone and garnish with 2 batons of roasted rhubarb and a slice of room temperature candied kumquat.

marinated prunes

1 vanilla bean, split

250 grams prune juice

250 grams honey

500 grams whole prunes

1 sprig of thyme

prune foam

500 grams prune juice

1 vanilla bean, scraped

100 grams sugar

5 grams versa whip

1 gram citric acid

1 gram xanthan gum

garnish

Young lemongrass leaves

Freeze dried corn kernels

Prepare marinated prunes: Split the vanilla bean and add to a saucepot along with the prune juice and honey, bring to a boil. Place the prunes and thyme in a plastic container. Pour the hot prune juice over prunes and cover with a tight fitting lid or plastic wrap. Allow the mixture to cool to room temperature before transferring to the refrigerator.

Prepare prune foam: Combine all ingredients in a blender. Transfer mixture to a stand mixer fitted with a whisk and whip on high speed until stiff peaks form.

Assembly: Place a cornbread pudding disc on a small metal plate. Remove the acetate from two corn tuile squares. Place one square on top of the pudding and place underneath a salamander (broiler) until the tuile softens and wraps around the pudding. Flip the pudding over and place the second tuile on top and repeat the same process. Allow the pudding to cool so the tuile returns to a crispy state. Drizzle some crème anglaise on a plate. Place the cornbread pudding on top. Place a dollop of prune foam and a slice of marinated prune beside the pudding. Garnish with young lemongrass leaves and freeze dried corn kernels.

HARD TO FIND ITEMS AVAILABLE AT BAKING SUPPLY SHOPS OR FROM LEPICERIE.COM

crystallized anise hyssop

Small bunch of anise hyssop

1 egg white, lightly beaten with a fork

50 grams sugar

black pepper lace

212 grams sugar

46 grams all-purpose flour

100 grams almond flour

1 teaspoon finely ground black pepper

100 grams water

50 grams butter, melted

red currant sauce

170 grams red currant puree, divided

1 teaspoon agar-agar

Pinch of salt

50 grams simple syrup, plus extra if needed

Prepare anise hyssop: Lightly brush both sides of leaves with the egg white and sprinkle both sides with sugar. Place on a tray lined with parchment or wax paper to air dry.

Prepare black pepper lace: Preheat oven to 325°F. Combine sugar, both flours, and black pepper to the bowl of a stand mixer. Mix with the paddle attachment on low speed just to combine. While the mixer is running, stream in the water, then melted butter until well combined. Chill mixture for 30 minutes. Lightly spray a silpat lined baking sheet with nonstick spray. With a small palette knife, spread about 1/2 teaspoon amounts of batter into thin strips, about 2 x 1/4 inches, making sure to space them about 2 inches apart. Bake for 6 minutes or until golden brown. While still hot, invert silpat onto a flat surface and peel away the silpat from the tuiles. Keep flat to prevent them from breaking. Store in an airtight container up to 3 days before serving.

Prepare red currant sauce: Combine 70 grams of the puree and the agar-agar in a small bowl and set aside. Combine the remaining puree and salt in a heatproof bowl. Bring a small pot filled 1/3 with water to a boil and place the bowl on top (without touching the water). Once boiling, pour a 1/4 of the hot mixture into the bowl with the agar-agar mixture and whisk together. Pour this back into bowl and boil for 1 minute. Place the bowl on top of another bowl filled with ice water to chill. The mixture should be almost solid. Now break this up with a wooden spoon and put into a blender with 50 grams of simple syrup. Start blending on low, and continue turning up the speed, stirring every so often, until the sauce is smooth and shiny with a consistency similar to lemon curd. Add more syrup if the sauce is too thick. This can be made up to 3 days in advance and stored in a squeeze bottle the fridge.

Assembly: Stir pineapple soup to smooth and transfer to a serving pitcher. For each serving, reheat about a teaspoon of roasted pineapple in a small sauté pan or in the microwave. Turn the hot pineapple onto a paper towel lined plate to absorb any excess butter. Squeeze a small dot of red currant sauce just off center of the plate. Spoon a small dollop of basil foam next to and touching the red currant sauce. Place a crystallized hyssop leaf on top of the foam. In the center of the bowl, touching the sauce and foam, position the warm roast pineapple dice in a single layer. Working quickly, make a small quenelle of frozen yogurt and place on the warm pineapple. Top the yogurt with a black pepper tuile. Pour soup into bowl tableside.

Prepare raspberry filling: Mix the sugar and apple pectin together. In a heavy saucepan, bring raspberry puree to a boil, stir in sugar mixture gradually and cook, stirring constantly, until mixture begins to thicken. Add raspberries and cook for another 3 minutes; chill.

Prepare white chocolate mousse: Submerge the gelatin sheets in a bowl of cold water for 10 minutes; remove and squeeze out excess water. Fill a medium saucepot half-way with water, and bring to a light simmer. Place the whole egg and yolks in a medium heat-proof bowl and place on top of the pot (the bottom of the bowl should not touch the water). Whisk vigorously until thick, about 3-4 minutes. Remove from heat. In another medium heat-proof bowl, place the chocolate over a pot of simmering water and heat, stirring occasionally to form a smooth slightly thickened liquid. Then place the drained gelatin in a small heat-proof bowl and place over a pot of simmering water, to melt; set side. In an electric mixer fitted with a whisk attachment, whip the egg whites until soft peaks form. Then whip the heavy cream to soft peaks. In a larger bowl, combine egg mixture, chocolate and melted gelatin. Mix well. Gently fold egg whites and whipped cream into white chocolate mixture.

Assembly: Spread an even, thin layer of raspberry filling on top of cheesecake and top with sponge cake. Using a brush, soak cake evenly with about 1½ to 2 cups tres leches soaking liquid. Spread the top with a 1/4-inch thick layer of chocolate mousse. Freeze until solid. Unmold cake, with a slightly heated knife, cut into 1-inch squares. Brush each plate with some of the raspberry filling. Place one piece of cake in the center of the brush stroke. Top the cake with a curl of white chocolate standing in a dollop of the raspberry filling.

grapefruit pearls

150 grams fresh grapefruit juice, strained through a fine meshed strainer

100 grams fresh orange juice, strained through a fine meshed strainer

100 grams granulated sugar

3 grams agar-agar

.4 grams locust bean gum

Vegetable oil, cold

orange pearls

250 grams fresh orange juice, strained

100 grams granulated sugar

3 grams agar-agar

.4 grams locust bean gum

Vegetable oil, cold

lemon pearls

100 grams fresh orange juice, strained

75 grams fresh lemon juice, strained

100 grams granulated sugar

3 grams agar-agar

.4 grams locust bean gum

Vegetable oil, cold

Prepare grapefruit pearl base: Combine the grapefruit juice, orange juice, and sugar, gently warming to dissolve sugar. Reserve warm. To complete, mix the agar-agar and locust bean gum into 150 grams water; transfer to a small saucepan. Bring mixture to a boil, reduce heat and simmer for 2 to 3 minutes. Remove from heat and incorporate into the base. Using a squeeze bottle or syringe, drop the mixture into cold vegetable oil, allowing 5 to 10 minutes to set. Transfer pearls with a fine meshed skimmer into cool water to rinse, then remove and drain in a fine meshed sieve.

Prepare orange pearl base: Combine the orange juice, and sugar, gently warming to dissolve the sugar. Reserve warm. To complete, disperse the agar-agar and locust bean gum in 150 grams water; transfer to a small saucepan. Bring mixture to a boil, reduce heat and simmer for 2 to 3 minutes. Remove from heat and incorporate into the base. Drop the mixture into cold vegetable oil, allowing 5 to 10 minutes to set. Transfer pearls to cool water to rinse, then drain.

Prepare lemon pearl base: Combine the lemon juice, 75 grams water, lemon juice, and sugar, gently warming to dissolve the sugar. Reserve warm. To complete, disperse the agar-agar and locust bean gum in the water; transfer to a small saucepan. Bring mixture to a boil, reduce heat and simmer for 2 to 3 minutes. Remove from heat and incorporate into the base. Drop the mixture into cold vegetable oil, allowing 5 to 10 minutes to set. Transfer pearls to cool water to rinse, then drain.

Assembly: Once each chocolate cup and cream assembly has set, spoon onto each the complimentary pearls: Grapefruit Pearls on the Dark Chocolate and Earl Grey, Orange Pearls on the Milk Chocolate and Star Anise, and Lemon Pearls on the Caramelized White Chocolate.

HARD TO FIND ITEMS AVAILABLE THROUGH LEPICERIE.COM

raspberry sauce

⅓ cup raspberry puree

1 teaspoon sugar

1 teaspoon pectin

garnish

½ pint fresh raspberry

Gold leaf

Pistachio nuts, halved

Prepare raspberry sauce: Bring the puree, sugar, and pectin to a boil, cool. Pour into a squeeze bottle or plastic pastry bag.

Assemble: On each plate, put a rectangle of brittany shortbread, place a piece of tuile on top of the shortcake, followed by a rectangle of the lemon sorbet, and finish the stack with another tuile rectangle. Carefully, place 6 raspberry side by side with a sugar decoration on top and a piece of the white chocolate mousse resting inside the sugar coil. Dot some raspberry sauce on plate. Garnish with a gold leaf and half a pistachio.

graham cracker crust

6 tablespoons (¾ stick) butter

2 tablespoons dark brown sugar

2 tablespoons sugar

2 tablespoons honey

1½ cups flour

¼ cup whole wheat flour

½ tablespoon salt

½ tablespoon cinnamon

cinnamon ganache

¼ cup cream

1 cinnamon stick

¼ cup sugar

1 tablespoon butter

3 ounces bittersweet chocolate

¼ teaspoon vanilla

¼ teaspoon salt

marshmallow fluff

4 egg whites

¾ cup plus 1 tablespoon sugar, divided

1¼ cups corn syrup

s'more pie

Prepare graham cracker crust: Preheat the oven to 350°F. In stand mixer cream the butter, both sugars and honey. Stir together dry ingredients and add to butter mixture. Mix just until combined. Gather dough together and roll to ¼ inch thick. Using a 2-inch cookie cutter, cut out 10 rounds of dough, chill rounds for 5 to 10 minutes. Line 10 – 1¾ inch pie pans with the rounds of dough being sure to press the dough into the bottom edges of the pans. Using baking beans or another pie pan, weigh down the dough and bake for approximately 20 minutes. Let cool completely.

Prepare cinnamon ganache: Heat cream with cinnamon stick to a simmer, set aside. Combine sugar and two tablespoons water in a saucepan and cook to an amber caramel. Strain cream into caramel and whisk to combine. Stir in the butter. Pour mixture over the chocolate and gently stir. Add salt and vanilla.

Prepare marshmallow fluff: Whip egg whites in a stand mixer with the whisk attachment. Once egg whites are foamy add one tablespoon sugar. In a saucepan, cook the remaining ¾ cup sugar, corn syrup, and ¼ cup water to a soft ball stage (235°F-240°F). Cautiously pour sugar mixture into egg whites while whipping. Continue whipping until cool. Store, covered in a dry container until ready to use.

Assemble pies: Pipe or spoon ganache into the prebaked pie shells. Let set at room temperature or place in refrigerator for 20 minutes. Pipe 3 dots of fluff on top of each pie. Toast fluff under a broiler for 2 to 3 minutes. Serve immediately.

Prepare diplomat cream: In a small saucepot, bring the milk and vanilla to a simmer. In a separate bowl, whisk the egg yolk and sugar together until pale and thick. Remove the pot of milk from the heat and slowly whisk in 1/3 of the hot milk into the egg mixture, then whisk the warm egg mixture back to the pot. Add the flour and cornstarch and cook until the mixture thickens (about 3 minutes). Transfer the mixture to a mixing bowl with a paddle attachment and mix on medium speed (no need to strain the mixture). Add the cold butter slowly until fully incorporated into the mixture. Cover with a sheet of plastic wrap and set aside to cool completely. In a bowl of an electric mixer, whip the heavy cream to medium peaks. Fold the whipped cream into the cooled thickened cream mixture in three additions, then add the lime zest. Transfer to a pastry bag and keep chilled until ready to use.

Assembly: Thinly slice approximately 4 fresh strawberries and arrange them overlapping along the insides of four 2 inch ring molds. Pipe the center of each mold with diplomat cream 3/4 full and top pieces of fresh strawberries, whole raspberries, blueberries, and blackberries. Place one of the meringue discs on each plate. Place the filled ring mold in the center of the disc and carefully slide off the mold. Spoon strawberry syrup around meringue disc. Serve with a scoop of basil-lime sorbet and decorate the plate with dabs of lemon curd, dots of meringue, and strawberry syrup.

ginger gelato

1¾ cup plus 2 tablespoons milk

1 cup cream (35% fat)

½ cup plus two tablespoons milk powder

½ cup dextrose powder

¾ cup sugar

1½ tablespoons ice cream stabilizer

1 tablespoon plus 1 teaspoon ginger puree

2 tablespoons plus 1 teaspoon candied ginger (small cubes)

Prepare ginger gelato: In a small saucepot, heat the milk, cream, milk powder and dextrose to 95°F. Add sugar and ice cream stabilizer and heat to 178°F. Transfer the liquid to a bowl or container set over another bowl of ice water, and stir occasionally until well chilled. Add ginger puree to cold base. Strain though a fine meshed sieve; churn base in gelato machine; fold chopped candy into gelato while extracting. Store frozen.

Plating: Cut paradiso into a rectangle about 3 inches long by 1/2 inch wide by 1/4 inch thick. Cut gelée the same dimensions and lay gelée on top of paradiso cake. Using a demitasse (espresso) spoon, make 4 quenelles of the lychee black tea cremoso and rest each on a slight angle atop of the gelée, making sure all are in a row, uniform and equal distance from one another. Using a square ice cream scooper, place a scoop of the ginger ice cream at the left end of the paradiso cake, so the ice cream rests against the edge of the cake. Gently place a 3-inch strand of cocoa mikado on top of the quenelles, allowing the left edge of the mikado to rest against the gelato, so the mikado barely pierces the gelato. Place a chocolate garnish against the left side of the gelato.

meyer lemon sorbet

1 quart Meyer lemon juice

1½ cups light corn syrup

1 cup simple syrup

cranberry caramel

¼ cup sugar

2 tablespoons orange juice

187 grams cranberries

citrus marmalade

5 oranges, segmented

4 lemons, segmented

1 grapefruit, segmented

¼ vanilla bean

Salt and sugar

garnish

Shaved fennel

Pomegranate seeds

Fresh orange and grapefruit segments

White chocolate pieces

Prepare lemon sorbet: Combine lemon juice, corn syrup, and simple syrup in a tall container using a hand immersion blender. Spin the base in your ice cream machine according to the manufacturer's instructions. Chill in freezer for 1 hour before serving.

Prepare cranberry caramel: In a medium saucepan over medium heat, bring the sugar with just enough water to cover to a simmer and place a bowl of ice water on the side. Continue to cook until the sugar is a light amber caramel color. Slowly add the orange juice to the caramel (being careful-it may spatter). Add cranberries and continue to cook until the cranberries are just tender. Transfer to a blender and blend until smooth. Strain through a fine meshed sieve into a bowl or container and set over the bowl of ice water; stir occasionally until well chilled.

Prepare citrus marmalade: Combine fruit segments; strain away any extra juice. Cook segments in a saucepan over medium heat, until they have broken down and the natural sugars have started to lightly caramelize. Remove from heat and add the vanilla bean, sugar and salt. Cover with a sheet of plastic wrap, adhering directly to the surface. Chill for at least one hour.

Assembly: Approximately one hour before serving, unmold the lemon mousses and transfer to the refrigerator. Place a white chocolate garnish on top of the mousse. Spoon a dollop of citrus marmalade on top of the white chocolate garnish. Along side the mousse, put together a salad of the shaved fennel, pomegranate, fresh orange and grapefruit. Make a small quenelle of the sorbet and spoon on top of salad. Garnish plate with cranberry caramel as a sauce.

pineapple gelée

1 fresh pineapple (for juicing)

4 sheets gelatin

¼ cup sugar

2 grams (a tiny pinch) fine sea salt

¼ gram (a very tiny pinch) citric acid

2 grams (a tiny pinch) Tahitian vanilla

pineapple sorbet

2 fresh pineapple (for juicing)

⅔ cup simple syrup (2:1; sugar to water)

3 grams (a pinch) fine sea salt

pineapple chip with thai basil

1 pineapple, peeled

30 medium-size Thai basil leaves, picked from their stems

Powdered sugar

grapefruit coulis

¾ cup plus 1 tablespoon fresh pink grapefruit juice

1 gram (a tiny pinch) xanthan gum

½ gram (a very tiny pinch) fine sea salt

Prepare pineapple gelée: Peel, chop and puree one pineapple to yield 1¼ cups of strained pineapple juice. Submerge the gelatin sheets in a bowl of cold water for 10 minutes; remove and squeeze out excess water. In a medium sized saucepot over low heat, gently warm the fresh pineapple juice, sugar, citric acid, salt, and vanilla to just below a simmer. Stir in the gelatin until dissolved. Pour the gelée onto a lipped baking tray; refrigerate until set. Cut 8 to 10 rounds with same ring cutter used for the curd.

Prepare pineapple sorbet: Peel and puree enough pineapple to yield 1 quart of strained pineapple juice. Add simple syrup and sea salt and whisk until evenly combined. Refrigerate overnight, then spin on an ice cream machine according to manufacturer's instructions.

Prepare pineapple chip: Preheat over to 200°F. Slice 10 to 20 rounds of pineapple, about 1/8 inch thick. Place half of the slices on to a sheet pan lined with a silpat sprayed with non-stick spray and lightly coated with powdered sugar. On each slice of pineapple, place a Thai basil leaf. Lightly sprinkle with powdered sugar. Place the other half of the pineapple slices on top. Finish by sprinkling more powdered sugar. Transfer the tray of chips to oven. Dry the chips about 90 minutes, until they become a light golden brown. If using a dehydrator, set at four, can take up to two days. When pineapple chips are still warm cut smaller rounds using a heavy gauge ring cutter to achieve a clean circle.

Prepare grapefruit coulis: Place grapefruit juice into a blender and cover with lid. Turn blender on medium speed and then remove lid. Slowly sprinkle the xanthan gum and salt into the grapefruit juice. Blend for two minutes, allowing the xanthan gum to hydrate. Strain through a fine mesh strainer and store in an airtight plastic container, chilled.

Plating: For each serving, place a small round disc of the tropical fruit on to the center of the plate. On a metal plate, stack one disc of baked brick dough, followed by a disc of lemon curd then a disc of pineapple gelée. Finish by topping with another disc of tropical fruit. Lift the stack off of the metal plate and place it directly on top of the base of tropical fruit. Carefully place a small quenelle of pineapple sorbet on top of the fruit. Stand one pineapple chip in the sorbet. Decorate the plate with the grapefruit coulis and basil oil.

Prepare candied coriander seeds: In a small saucepot, bring the sugar and 2½ cups water to a boil, making simple syrup; set aside. Fill another pot with water along with the coriander seeds; bring to a boil. Once it has boiled, strain the water from the seeds and repeat twice. Add the blanched seeds into the simple syrup. On low heat, let the syrup boil with the seeds until it thickens. Strain the seeds and spread onto a silpat. Dry in the 180°F oven overnight.

To serve: Dip a 2 inch round cookie cutter in warm water and cut out rounds of pudding #1. Place rounds onto a siltpat. Place the cutout pudding rings on each plate. Transfer pudding #2 into a pastry bag and pipe a nice round pile on the top of pudding #1 just off center. Sprinkle 3 coriander seeds on top of the soft pudding. Just off to the side, scoop a small quenelle of the sorbet, and garnish with the lemon glass and a small sprig of micro mint. Sprinkle the lemon shortcrust around the bottom of the pudding.

chocolate espresso pudding

1 quart plus ⅔ cup milk, divided

1 cup sugar, divided

Pinch of salt

4 tablespoons cocoa powder

2 tablespoons cornstarch

2 eggs plus 4 egg yolks

10 ounces bittersweet chocolate, chopped

4 tablespoons butter

1 tablespoon plus 1 teaspoon vanilla extract

2 tablespoons coffee extract, preferably Trablit

garnish (as needed)

Espresso syrup*

Chocolate cigarettes

Powdered sugar

Prepare chocolate espresso pudding: In a medium saucepot, bring 1 quart of the milk, 1/2 cup sugar, and salt to a boil. In a bowl, combine the cocoa powder, cornstarch and remaining 2/3 cup milk; whisk until it resembles a paste. In a separate bowl, whisk together the eggs, egg yolks and remaining 1/2 cup sugar. Melt chocolate and butter; add both extracts. When milk reaches a boil, add the cocoa mixture and whisk until thickened. Whisk into the egg mixture and return to heat and cook until thick. Remove from heat and mix in the melted chocolate mixture (ganache). Strain through a fine meshed sieve onto a large baking pan. Cover the surface with a sheet of plastic wrap to avoid the development of a skin, and chill.

Assembly: In the bottom of a large burgundy glass, place 2 triangles of the candied orange peel, and 3 pieces of candied figs. Drizzle fudge sauce and a reduction of the fig poaching liquid into glass. Pipe whipped cream into one side of the base of the glass. Place tuile in glass, using whipped cream to help support it. Pipe chocolate pudding into tuile, filling nearly full. Moisten top of pudding with sweet espresso syrup. Push two chocolate cigarettes into pudding. Heavily dredge with powdered sugar.

*ONE ESPRESSO WITH AN EQUAL MEASURE OF SUGAR

Prepare walnut nougatine: Combine sugar and lemon juice in a small saucepan. Cook over medium heat without stirring, until sugar in melting and beginning to caramelize. Stir with a wooden spoon, until all sugar is melted, and a light caramel color is achieved. Stir in walnuts, and coat them completely, pour onto a lightly oiled baking sheet. Set aside to cool. Break up into random pieces. The nougatine can be stored in a sealed container at room temperature for several weeks.

Plating: Cut carrot cake into 12 rectangular pieces, 1½ inch x 3 inch diameter. Place one piece of cake on each plate with one piece of walnut nougatine standing upright. Grind the remaining walnut nougatine into a powder. Place some powered walnut nougatine to the right of cake with a quenelle of toasted walnut ice cream on top. Sprinkle a little powered walnut nougatine on top of the ice cream. Using an immersion blender, holding at an angle to incorporate air, aerate carrot juice to make a foam and use to garnish plate.

Prepare caramel sauce: Cook the water, corn syrup and sugar in a heavy-sided saucepan over medium heat until it reaches a deep amber color. Stir once or twice while cooking. As color begins to appear, swirl mixture by rotating pan to ensure even caramelization. Turn off heat, and slowly whisk cream into the caramel. Be careful as cream may spatter and the caramel will give off a lot of steam. Whisk the mixture smooth. If not smooth, return to low heat, and continue to whisk. Remove from heat and add the salt, whisking until dissolved. Set aside at room temperature until ready to use.

Prepare almond nougatine: Preheat oven to 325°F. Line a baking sheet with a silpat and set aside. In a small saucepot, combine the sugar, butter and corn syrup. Cook on low heat until butter is melted and sugar dissolved. Remove from heat, and whisk in flour and salt. Stir in chopped almonds. Set aside until batter is cool enough to handle. Once cool, spoon teaspoon size drops of the batter onto silpat about 2 inches apart. Bake until a deep golden brown, about 6 to 8 minutes. Cool to room temperature. When ready to serve, carefully remove the cookies from the silpat, as they are very thin and delicate.

Assembly: For each serving, place a disc of espresso-almond shortbread cookie onto a small plate. Dip the espresso semifreddo mold in warm water to loosen edges, then invert onto the shortbread. Drizzle top of semifreddo with the salted caramel sauce. Garnish with a piece of almond nougatine.